ART & STORY

ART & STORY

THE ROLE OF ILLUSTRATION IN MULTICULTURAL LITERATURE FOR YOUTH

THE VIRGINIA HAMILTON CONFERENCE

EDITED BY
ANTHONY L. MANNA
AND
CAROLYN S. BRODIE

KENT STATE UNIVERSITY

Highsmith PRESS

Fort Atkinson, Wisconsin

Published by Highsmith Press LLC
W5527 Highway 106
P.O. Box 800
Fort Atkinson, Wisconsin 53538-0800

The paper used in this publication meets the minimum requirements of American
National Standard for Information Science — Permanence of Paper for Printed
Library Material. ANSI/NISO Z39.48-1992.

Library of Congress Cataloging-in-Publication Data
Virginia Hamilton Conference (1997 : Kent State University)
    Art & story : the role of illustration in multicultural literature
for youth : the Virginia Hamilton Conference / edited by Anthony L.
Manna and Carolyn S. Brodie.
        p.   cm.
    Selected presentations from the conference.
    Includes bibliographical references and index.
    ISBN 0-917846-77-X (pbk. : alk. paper)
    1. Illustration of books--20th century--United States--Themes,
  motives--Congresses. 2. Illustrated books, Children's--United
  States--Themes, motives--Congresses. 3. Ethnicity in art--
Congresses. I. Manna, Anthony L. II. Brodie, Carolyn S. III. Title.
NC975.V57 1997
741.6'42'0973--dc21   97-11112
                                                              CIP

Art & Story is dedicated to the memory of our friend and fellow Virginia Hamilton Advisory Board member, Dan MacLachlan. We admired and miss his sense of humor, his wonderful strokes of genius, his constant support and his devotion to the Virginia Hamilton Conference.

America is for me a country of parallel cultures rather than the more traditional, narrower view that portrays it as a land of the majority surrounded by minorities. It is a country of parallel peoples, each creating a significant literature out of their own unique yet universal qualities. Therefore, it must be a land where all cultures and all ethnic groups are of equal value and of equal importance to our children, who are descendents of the world's peoples.

–Virginia Hamilton, ***Many Faces, Many Voices***
(Highsmith Press, 1992)

CONTENTS

PREFACE

ART AND STORY, our second book of presentations given at the Virginia Hamilton Conference, grew out of a question we'd been asking for some time: Have we as a profession given adequate attention to the role of illustration in multicultural books for young people? Once asked, that question generated many others. What types of visual images ought to matter to those of us who read, critique, and recommend books? How does book design, that is, the flow of the whole visual experience, reinforce the visual impact of individual illustrations? What have the conference illustrators and workshop leaders said about the aesthetics of picture book art? What have they said about the art of illustrated books that depict particular cultural themes and experiences? What claims have they made about the ways young readers make sense of these themes and experiences? Can multicultural illustrations do what Hazel Rochman, writing in the *Horn Book Magazine* of March/April 1995, suggests multicultural stories can do, namely, "...transform you because they help you imagine beyond yourself"?

To see if we had enough material on illustration to fill a book that addressed questions of this sort, we took stock of the topics and issues that the artists and workshop leaders have raised about illustrated books at the conference. To do this, we watched videotapes of the speeches that illustrators have made at the conference throughout its history—from the first conference of 1985 to the most recent of 1996—and we talked to members of the conference advisory board and others who had attended workshops that focused on illustration and book design. When we emerged from this review, we knew that the conference had given a lot of attention to the art of the illustrated book and kids' responses to it. In fact, we discovered that throughout the history of the conference there had been an ongoing dialogue about illustration and book design, and that this dialogue contained a strikingly rich reserve of material—claims, criticism, advice, concerns, and controversies about the nature and role of illustration and about how the images in illustrated books can promote multiculturalism, among other things. This book of selected presentations on the relationship between art and story was the result of our analysis.

While in the pages to follow the conference presenters may not explore all of our concerns about this topic, they clearly—and rigorously, we think—cast a bright light on many of them. Virginia Hamilton herself sets the tone for the chapters that follow in an interview that examines her views of the way art and language come together in her books to tell the whole story. She also describes her collaboration with some of the finest illustrators working in the field today. In the same illuminating vein, Arnold Adoff pays tribute to the interpretive skill of illustrators in a "poet's prose" piece that draws attention to the art Lisa Desimini did for one of his most recent collections of poems. The piece provides a rare look at actual correspondence between poet and artist.

Chapters by nine illustrators follow Arnold Adoff's interlude. Inviting us into their lives and studios, these illustrators talk about work habits, routines, technique, ways of approaching content and theme in visual terms, and the challenge they face in their effort to accurately interpret place, character, and event. In his chapter, an interview which elaborates and updates the keynote speech he made at the 1990 conference, Jerry Pinkney traces the key turns his career has taken, describes his obligation to get every detail culturally and historically right, and reveals how he literally dramatizes the raw material of a text in order to bring to visual life its special features. In her chapter, Pat Cummings also attends to her development. In her case, however, she describes an evolution that's intricately linked to memories of a happy and eventful family life and to experiences she had growing up, as she puts it, as an "army brat" who traveled the world over. She proposes that if her books attract kids, it's because the situations and characters she both illustrates and writes about, though clearly set in a particular cultural community, present them with universal themes to which they can relate.

In the two chapters that follow, Floyd Cooper's "Exploring Cultures: An Artist's Story" and Brian Pinkney's "The Rhythm of My Art," the illustrators elaborate on the demands of melding medium and "message," of finding a visual metaphor that complements the mood and tone of the written text, but which, at the same time, broadens it—*interprets* it—by telling more than the words do.

In the next chapter, Vera B. Williams discusses two of the most significant themes that drive her work: the desire for community and the need for hope. She discloses how she uses color, design, space, and character relationships to translate these universal urges into the particulars of a culture.

Shonto Begay's discussion, in the chapter that's titled "Reflections from a Holy Space," follows a similar tact. He discusses how he sets both his aesthetic and his politics within the context of the community into which he was born and which to this day feeds his imagination—a Navajo reservation. Drawing on Navajo traditions and spiritual beliefs and practices, Mr. Begay describes—sometimes very humorously—the disjunction in his community between past and present and shows how this tension often informs specific aspects of his art.

The next two chapters move directly into the heart of cultural matters. Lulu Delacre's "A Latina Building Bridges" focuses on the traditional motifs she uses to ensure cultural authenticity in her books of Puerto Rican songs, chants, tales, myths, and legends, and Patricia Polacco's "Heroes" addresses the personal experiences and memories, especially fond family memories for which she seems to have instant recall, that shape her sense of the diverse cultures which she depicts in all of her picture books. Ms. Polacco makes it clear that as a writer and illustrator she feels comfortable moving among many cultures because she cares deeply for her characters and what happens to them.

Finally, in a series of stirring vignettes that reveals his process as an illustrator, James Ransome discusses the work that consumes him when he makes a picture book. For Mr. Ransome the process begins with an exhaustive study of a manuscript, continues with painstaking research and experimentation, and ends with risky decisions about form, fact, and feeling.

No book that proposes to deal with the discussions about illustration that have taken place at the Virginia Hamilton Conference would be complete without reference to the workshops that have evoked so much rich dialogue at the conference. The four workshops that are represented here did just that—as the essays on which they are based demonstrate.

In the first essay, Dianne Hess, of Scholastic Press, provides an editor's perspective on which multicultural books get published. After describing criteria that guide her decisions about the manuscripts that cross her desk, Ms. Hess focuses on a sampling of multicultural picture books that she has brought to publication. All of these books celebrate, as she puts it, particular "voices of America." Several of them are the work of illustrators whose presentations appear in this book.

In the next essay, "Updating the Race: Transformations in Racial Presentation Since 1975," Opal J. Moore examines various incongruities, misrepresentations, and misconceptions in a sampling of fiction—much of it otherwise critically acclaimed—that mines the history of what she calls "The Black Experience." Having done that, she explores several touchstone books on this experience, books that serve up balanced points of reference. These books, Ms. Moore suggests, offer us the types of cultural criteria that we can use when assessing the attitudes and dispositions that are rooted in written and illustrated texts of fiction on particular African American experiences.

The final two essays take us from home to communities around the world. In "All in My Family: Picture Books Reflecting Families' Cultural Diversity," Sue McCleaf Nespeca describes illustrated books that open windows to cultural diversity among families and in "How Do They Stack Up? Best Picture Books from Abroad," Maureen White shares her views on illustrated books that open windows to cultures outside the United States.

We conclude the book with four appendixes. The first, "A Listing of Selected Multicultural Trade Books for Children and Young Adults," describes over fifty recent notable books, representing various literary genres, that members of the Virginia Hamilton Conference Advisory Board recommend for their accurate and authentic depictions of cultural experiences. The second, "A Multicultural Media Festival," also describes notable material, in this instance, films, videotapes, and CD-ROMs that invite us to observe styles of life around the corner and around the world. The third appendix focuses on the annual Virginia Hamilton Essay Award. It contains a description of the award, the criteria used to select the winning essay, and a listing of the writers who have so far won the award. The final appendix traces that history of the Virginia Hamilton Conferences.

ACKNOWLEDGMENTS

In more ways than we can mention, the Virginia Hamilton Conference is a collaborative event, and we have many people and organizations to thank for their encouragement and generous support. To acknowledge with any thoroughness all the people and organizations that have helped with this book and with the conference throughout its thirteen-year history would require a separate and lengthy chapter. With our apologies then to any of our collaborators whom we forget to mention here, we gratefully acknowledge the following people, programs, and agencies for their assistance:

Publishers that generously waived their standard fee when they gave us permission to reprint material from their books in this book: Greenwillow Books, HarperCollins, North-South Books, Philomel Books, and Scholastic Press.

Members of the current Virginia Hamilton Conference Advisory Board, who never stint on terrific advice and remarkable dedication, despite their hectic schedules: Gloria Brown, East Cleveland Public Library; Ione Cowen, Akron-Summit County Public Library; Darwin Henderson, University of Cincinnati; Nora Kegley, Kent, Ohio; Bonnie Kelly, Cuyahoga County Public Library's Strongsville Branch; Yvette Kirksey, Akron City Schools; John Marcelino, Orange City Schools; Deborah McHamm, A Cultural Exchange, Cleveland; Sue McCleaf Nespeca, NOLA Regional Library System; Janice Smuda, Cuyahoga County Public Library; Dave Tirpak, Orange City Schools; and Jan Wojnaroski, Kent City Schools.

The College of Continuing Studies staff for their stunning attention to the finest details and for keeping us on task on time: Lori Gourley, Program Coordinator; Laura Dees; Candace Grace; Teresa Josof.

For continuing generous funding support: Akron-Summit County Public Library; Cuyahoga County Public Library; Hamilton Arts, Inc.; Highsmith Press; NOLA Regional Library System; and Victor C. Laughlin, M. D. Memorial Foundation Trust.

For providing financial assistance to help us get started: The Cleveland Foundation and The George Gund Foundation.

Kent State University colleagues and friends who helped with funding, great ideas, and plenty of humor: Tom Barber, former Dean, College of Fine and Professional Arts; Nancy Birk, Associate Curator, Special Collections and Archives; Marlene Dorsey, Dean, College of Continuing Studies; Pris Drach (for graciously welcoming us into her home); Chuck Kegley, former Chair, Department of Adult, Counseling, Health, and Vocational Education (for graciously welcoming us into his home); Jeanne Somers, Curator, Special Collections and Archives; Danny Wallace, Director, School of Library and Information Science; Joanne Rand Whitmore, Dean, College of Education; and Clis Stauffer, Karen Steiner, and Pauli Stewart, Department of Teaching, Leadership, and Curriculum Studies.

Don Sager, Publisher, Highsmith Press, for knowing that there's art in story and story in art.

Janet Hill, Old Trail School, editor extraordinaire, for showing us how to read between the lines.

Janet Loch, School of Library and Information Science, for transcribing challenging videotapes with such care and patience.

The many conference presenters for sharing their talent and wisdom.

And many special thanks to the featured speakers and workshop presenters who so graciously gave us permission to publish their illuminating work.

ABOUT VIRGINIA HAMILTON

THE RECIPIENT OF every major award and honor in her field, Virginia Hamilton is one of today's most distinguished writers for children and young adults. She was the first African American woman to win the coveted Newbery Award for "the most distinguished contribution to literature for children" for *M. C. Higgins, the Great*, for which she also won the National Book Award and the *Boston Globe-Horn Book* Award. Three other books, *The Planet of Junior Brown; Sweet Whispers, Brother Rush;* and *In the Beginning*, a collection of creation myths from around the world, have been named Newbery Honor books. In addition, Ms. Hamilton has twice been awarded a Certificate of Honor by the International Board on Books for Young People, and she has received the Coretta Scott King Award four times, most recently for *Her Stories: African American Folktales, Fairy Tales*, and *True Tales*. She also is the recipient of the *Boston Globe-Horn Book* Award for *Sweet Whispers, Brother Rush* and *Anthony Burns: The Defeat and Triumph of a Fugitive Slave*, a biography. She has also won the Mystery Writers of America Edgar Award for *The House of Dies Drear. Cousins*, a novel praised by *Booklist* for "...astonishing moments of betrayal and redemption," was selected a Best Book of 1990 by *Parenting Magazine*, a Best Book for Young Adults by the American Library Association, and a Pick of the Lists by *American Bookseller. Arilla Sun Down*, singled out by *Kirkus Reviews* for its "dazzling, uncommon impact," was named a *School Library Journal* Best Book of the Year.

Other awards and honors have followed. In 1990 Ms. Hamilton received both an honorary doctorate from the Bank Street College of Education and the Regina Medal from the Catholic Library Association. In 1992 she was awarded the Hans Christian Andersen Author Award, which is given by the International Board on Books for Young People to a living author whose works have made a significant contribution to children's literature. In its citation, the IBBY states, "Virginia Hamilton's work has been recognized in her native country and through numerous translations abroad for its profound humanity, breathtaking depth and complexity, and innovative and poetic use of language, especially the vernacular of Black America." In 1993 she was invited to deliver the May Hill Arbuthnot Honor Lecture by the American Library Association. In 1995 she received the Laura Ingalls Wilder Medal for her lasting contribution to literature for children, and in the same year she became the first children's book author to have been awarded a "genius grant" as a fellow of the John D. and Catherine T. MacArthur Foundation.

Virginia Hamilton was born into the flat, rural landscape of Ohio farm country, where her mother's family had lived since the late 1850s, when Ms. Hamilton's grandfather, Levi Perry, escaped from slavery on the Underground Railroad. She now resides in Yellow Springs, Ohio, with her husband, acclaimed poet and anthologist Arnold Adoff, on land that has been in her family for generations.

About writing, Virginia Hamilton has said, "Language is magic, has always been magic, since the time sorcerers uttered their incantations…. I am a believer in language and its magic monarchy! To bind its boundless spell is why I write."

When Birds Could Talk and Bats Could Sing by Virginia Hamilton, illustrated by Barry Moser.

1

REFLECTIONS ON THE ILLUSTRATOR'S ROLE
AN INTERVIEW WITH VIRGINIA HAMILTON
ANTHONY L. MANNA AND CAROLYN S. BRODIE

SOME OF THE MOST distinguished illustrators of our time have graced Virginia Hamilton's texts with their art. As a writer in search of illustrators who share her deep respect for the struggles and triumphs of African Americans, Virginia Hamilton has—for over 30 years now—enlisted the extraordinary talents and passionate attention of a highly respected and prized company of artists: Floyd Cooper, Leo and Diane Dillon, Nonny Hogrogian, Barry Moser, Jerry Pinkney, and others. Their collaborations have offered up an elaborate cultural duet on the page, with the pictures and other visual elements providing stunning interpretive images that work in tandem with the writer's invigorating and poetic style. These images enrich and illuminate her vibrant portraits of the soul of black America.

In her many discussions about her work, Virginia Hamilton has rarely focused exclusively on her partnership with her illustrators. In this interview, then, we invited her to address the illustrator's role in her books and her feelings about the vision of culture her illustrators have brought to her texts. We spoke with Virginia Hamilton in early March 1996, in her home in Yellow Springs, Ohio, a former station of the Underground Railroad, where five generations of her family have resided.

M/B: What do you think the illustrator's responsibility is when working with a text which you've written?

VH: To begin with, illustrators should be true to their art. But, given the form they're working in, they also need to respond in kind to the particular textures of the text they're presented with. The illustrators I work with are so extraordinary that their response is always appropriate. This is the reason why I leave them to their own devices most of the time. I believe in their art, and I know what they're capable of, and they rise to the occasion of my texts. I seem to get some of the finest work out of illustrators. In fact, reviewers and critics of my books often say that this is the best artwork so and so has done, the most accessible, and so forth.

M/B: Do you collaborate with the illustrator once a book is underway?

VH: The process of fitting the artwork to the text begins as soon as I have a firm concept for a book. Now with *Her Stories*, for example, the process was really hurried. As it turned out, I put together a manuscript larger than was economically feasible to publish, and all of us were working under a very tight deadline. The Dillons had to have the stories while I was still working on them and my editor and I were still choosing which ones to include in the book. So I would complete a few stories and rush them off to my editor. The Dillons may well have illustrated several stories that weren't included in the book because of space constraints. You've no doubt noticed that the illustrations in the latter part of the book are different from the others. The ones near the end are like little portraits. There just wasn't enough time for them to do the detailed pictures that are found throughout most of the book. Actually, those little portraits work beautifully, though they're set in a different format than the others.

M/B: Once you send off a manuscript to your editor, are you usually given an opportunity to give your opinion about the illustrator's renderings? How involved are you in the process of putting a book together?

VH: The editor is always in the middle of any negotiating once a book is underway. She knows us all very well, and all of us have enormous trust in her, just as we trust one another. But there are occasions when it's necessary to talk about the fit between the illustrations and the text I've written. With *Her Stories*, for example, Leo Dillon asked if I would be willing to change a small part of the text, because he and Diane had completed the illustration that accompanied the text prior to a change I had made in the writing. I altered the section in question because it was just a matter of a few words. In another case with *Her Stories*, the Dillons gave the fairy story "Mom Bett and the Little Ones A-Glowing" an interpretation I questioned at first. They cast the fairies in an Egyptian mode. I was a little put off by this at first sight, because in my mind I saw Western-type fairies with wings and such. But the more I looked at the Dillons' concept, the more I could see that it made perfect visual sense. Although situations like these do arise from time to time, most of the time illustrators discover their own sense of my books without any input from me. Whenever I do research for a book, though, as I did with *Her Stories*, I'm in the habit of sharing at least some of the research with my illustrators, knowing that they'll do more research if they see a need.

M/B: Have you ever rejected the artwork for one of your books?

VH: Yes, I have.

M/B: Do you ever have a say in choosing an illustrator?

VH: I work that out with the editor as soon as the project is conceived. For example, when I first came up with the idea for the *Her Stories* book, Bonnie Verburg, my editor at Scholastic, asked me if I had an illustrator in mind. She named several illustrators who might work well, but she agreed to approach the Dillons once I told her they would be perfect for the book.

M/B: And that was before a word was written?

VH: That's right.

M/B: So you're pretty much in control from the beginning.

VH: Yes, I do have the option to say what illustrator I would very much like. I knew from the very start that I wanted Barry Moser to illustrate *When Birds Could Talk and Bats Could Sing*.

M/B: Why is that?

VH: Because I believe he is the greatest watercolorist working in children's books today. You see, I think of the book as a whole, which means that I know which illustrator can make the book come alive visually. First of all, Barry was raised in the South, and the stories in *When Birds Could Talk and Bats Could Sing* are based on African American folktales told in the South during the plantation era. I knew he'd adore those stories, and he did. He started painting almost from the moment he read them and kept painting until he had completed nearly 40 watercolors. I understand from Bonnie Verburg that only a small number were ever changed from the original renderings. His first thought for the design of the book was to make the whole book about four inches high, a small pocket book to fit in the hand of a small child, which is a sweet idea. The book, of course, is quite a lot bigger than that. We laugh a lot about how it kept growing. All the birds are anatomically and scientifically correct, except that they wear hats, which is a marvelous touch. And their expressions are hysterical. There's an interesting story behind the development of Barry's wonderful painting of the boy Alcee holding the pumpkin in the opening tale, "How Bruh Sparrow and Sis Wren Lost Out." The text reads, "...Alcee tore the pumpkin from the vine. He held it in his arms and strolled off across the field. Sadly, Sis Wren and Bruh Sparrow watched him go." Originally, I wrote it so that he put the pumpkin under his arm, but Barry responded by saying that he couldn't show Alcee carrying off such a large pumpkin that way, and would I change the text to fit the action. As you see, that's what I did, because in this case it didn't hurt the text at all to make the change. In fact, it added to the drama of the story.

M/B: When you have discussions like this, do you actually talk with the illustrator directly or do you work through your editor?

VH: It depends. Sometimes, but not in that instance. I usually talk with Barry Moser directly because we know each other very well. And that's the way it's been from the very beginning, when he did the illustrations for *The All Jahdu Storybook*. He's an extraordinary human being. To give you an example of a big change he's made in his work, take a look at his full-page spread of the peacock in "Still and Ugly Bat" in *When Birds Could Talk and Bats Could Sing*. In the past, Barry didn't use to like to have an illustration cross the gutter of a book. In fact, he wouldn't do this at first. So, in a way, what you have when you don't move into the book's gutter are less vigorous portraits than you have when you do cross the gutter. There's much more movement to an illustration that uses the large space of the page that way. It's a risky thing to do, though, because it splits the image and could distort it. But as you can see in the picture of the peacock, Barry uses the entire page brilliantly. No distortion whatsoever.

M/B: Mr. Moser seems to have had a lot of fun with these stories. There's such a sense of playfulness about the entire enterprise.

VH: There's a lot to play with. For one thing, there are all sorts of verses and songs in these tales, because they're written in the *cante fable* tradition. What this means is that in addition to rhymes and songs, there's a moral at the end of each of the stories, which makes them that much more interesting. The moral that concludes "How Bruh Sparrow and Sis Wren Lost Out" reads, "So, children, here's a leaf from the book of birds: *Pick on your own size. For it's no use squabbling over what's too big for you to handle.*" I made the morals stronger than the ones I found in the original tales I was working with for this book, and that strength is due partly to the way I position myself as a narrator who talks directly to children. The morals were great fun to work with.

M/B: Where did you find these stories?

VH: That's a story in itself. I was doing research for another project when a research helper happened upon these tales quite by accident. She didn't realize what she'd found, but I recognized their value at once. The stories I tell in the book are based on African American folktales told in the South during the plantation era. In the 1800s one Martha Young, a white journalist who sometimes wrote under a pseudonym, collected them and created many of her own, publishing them in newspapers and in several collections of folktales. She was three years old at the end of the Civil War, and her family's former slaves became the paid servants of her wealthy household. Martha Young was an extraordinary collector of black folktales, songs, and sayings, and she became a very popular "dialect interpreter." We have no way of knowing what she sounded like doing so-called black dialect at the turn of the century, but she became quite famous. She sold out Carnegie Hall and was reviewed very favorably by the *New York Times* and other newspapers. Then she completely disappeared. All of her books were out of print. They have been dead for over half a century.

M/B: Do you know why that happened?

VH: Joel Chandler Harris and the Uncle Remus stories is why. His work with animal stories was so powerful that he completely dwarfed her.

M/B: And you respect her effort?

VH: Of course I can't possibly know how she felt about black people, but from what I can tell from her treatment of the tales, I assume she respected the folks from whom she collected them. Still, there were times when she used the term *darkie*. She was, after all, a woman of her time. We are no longer able to know which were her own stories in the African American tradition and which she heard from black tellers. But having resurrected them, I felt I had a duty to take them back, even hers, because they are all beautiful and I hear the voices of black tellers in them and even the imitative voice of Martha Young. I recast these stories for young people in a colloquial language that reads and sounds equally well. They were written down in a fractured English, part Gullah, part I don't know what.

M/B: In the illustrations, each of the animals has a distinct personality.

VH: As I said, Barry Moser fell in love with the stories. We differed, though, on clothing the animals. The animals in *The People Could Fly* have no clothes, as I requested they not have to Leo and Diane Dillon, who illustrated it, and they agreed. Since Barry would have clothes and I would not, we compromised. Each bird and bat wears a hat which really contributes to the animal's personality.

M/B: When you're working on a book which will be illustrated, do you consider the visual images which eventually will enhance the writing? Are you a visual writer?

VH: I am a visual writer, but it's not illustrations that I visualize. The characters and action are what I visualize. And, of course, I know my craft and form. With picture books I know there has to be something there for somebody to illustrate. Particularly in a book like *When Birds Could Talk and Bats Could Sing,* I make sure my language is full of description and detail so that the illustrator can take off on that. Not so specific that the writing will restrict the illustrator, but enough detail for an illustrator to play with. It's a matter of leaving enough room in the language and enough room between the people.

M/B: You said that you know the craft of the picture book. How would you describe that craft, that form?

VH: To answer that, I'd first have to say that with my books, the main thing is the writing. Illustrators come to my books and must fit into my work. If the main thing is the writing, then it's the writer's book. So I start out thinking only of the writing. When I began to conceptualize *Her Stories,* I was thinking about my mother, whom I missed, and the stories she told.

All of a sudden the book became an entity in my head. "Ah ha," I said, "I've never done a collection of traditional stories that looks exclusively at females." When I'm working with folk material like the tales I gathered for this book and for *The People Could Fly,* I'm actually recasting them, composing them anew in my own written-down style of telling. If you could compare my versions of these narratives with the raw material I work with, you'd see something of the process that goes into transforming the original sources into stories that read well both on the page and out loud. When I'm reshaping them, I'm also aware that they are going to be illustrated and how they are going to be illustrated. I want to be sure there are adequate visual details and visual action for the illustrator.

M/B: You never call yourself a "reteller."

VH: That's because I'm not a "reteller" of these tales, but a "teller." Sometimes reviewers will say "retold by Virginia Hamilton," but that's a misnomer. Look at the jackets of these collections and you'll see that "told by Virginia Hamilton" is the correct way to put it. After all, storytellers tell stories, and they tell them differently and uniquely each time they do. I believe that I've brought this kind of collection to a level it has never been brought to before. I actually recast the stories in a kind of colloquial speech that is also very literary and yet easy for anyone to read. I knew people would be reading these stories out loud to children, but that they would also be studied in college classrooms. I wanted them to have wide appeal, and to achieve that I had to spend a lot of time working on the language.

M/B: All of your illustrated books are neither picture storybooks nor chapter books. They seem to fit somewhere in between these two traditional forms.

VH: Well, my collections represent a traditional form—the anthology. *Jaguarundi* is a 32-page picture book. But I get what you mean. The form in *Drylongso* and *The Bells of Christmas* is my own. We call it a "Hamilton." It's what novelists do when they try to write a picture book! I started out wanting to do the illustrated books as standard 32-page picture books, but I couldn't do that because I found that I had too much to say. I had to come up with a picture book format that could integrate illustrations with a long story. And what emerged is the form you see in *Drylongso* and *The Bells of Christmas*. It suits perfectly a kind of writing I like to do occasionally, which is quite different from writing a novel.

M/B: What functions do the illustrations serve in the form you're describing?

VH: They open up the stories and invite you in. *Drylongso* is a good example of what I mean. When I wrote this story about a farming family, I had a locale like southern Texas in mind. Jerry Pinkney's illustrations for *Drylongso* so vividly portray the look and feel of that region of the country. He uses a white light and a sandy texture that capture the awful drought these people must endure. These visual elements greatly enhance the atmosphere of the story. Rarely does anyone write about black families in rural areas, so I hope the book broadens people's notions of the experiences of African Americans. It is only recently that half of the African American families haven't lived in rural areas, and many still do live on their own farms. It was this phenomenon I addressed in *Drylongso*, where I tell about a black family eking out an existence on an isolated farm during a terrible drought.

M/B: Throughout the years, have you seen many changes in the way your books are illustrated?

VH: I don't know if the changes are a matter of style or the increasing sophistication of children's books. Children's books in general have grown increasingly sophisticated to keep up with the sophistication of the readership. When you have three-year-olds working on computers, you have an obligation to live up to what they're learning. Kids are also reading voraciously, and good literature is getting into schools as it never has before. The more children see and the more they learn, the more sophisticated they become about artwork and text.

Now, in regard to the representation of African Americans in children's books, the changes have been very interesting. Since I started writing for young people, we've moved through a period when "Black is beautiful" was the sentiment to a period in history when separation and black nationalism were a rallying cry. At this point in time, we are embracing the strong influence that American blacks have had in this country, and this attitude, it seems to me, is so much wiser than the back-to-Africa feeling that was so dominant in an earlier time. What I like best about young African American illustrators is their freedom that knows no boundaries. They now work in every conceivable style, and they illustrate books by writers from many different cultures. There was a time when that would not have been possible, just as there was a time when only a black illustrator would have done a black author's book. Of course, I defied that kind of pigeonholing early on when Symeon Shimin illustrated *Zeely,* my first book. If anybody knows ordinary people it's someone who knows the Russian peasantry, as Shimin did. He did a wonderful job with *Zeely,* which proves a point.

Today we're seeing many examples of good, sensitive illustrators doing a fine job of working in cultures that are not their own. So the world of the illustrated book has opened up more to a diversity of voices. Of course, if you didn't have adventurous publishers like Scholastic and adventurous editors like Bonnie Verburg, none of these changes would be possible. We're witnessing a period of very fine bookmaking and book design. And the content is forever broadening. While it is still true that many children's books are created through the prism of popular culture, which tends to avoid the broad cultural foundation of this country, things are changing. I think that my books have been responsible for many of these changes, because I have broadened the field and a created a canon at the same time. Yes, there was a cultural children's literature before me, but there wasn't the diversity of genre and subject matter I've created in the more than 30 books I've published over the years. Nor has there been another writer for young people, black or white, who has done the amount of speaking and writing I've done about writing and my particular parallel culture. You can follow the history of my books through my published speeches. When you trace my history, you see that my books have widened the cultural landscape and provided a bridge to the past and between the generations.

M/B: Over the years, the Virginia Hamilton Conference has celebrated the work of many distinguished illustrators. What do you find most striking about their contribution?

VH: The extraordinary diversity and range of their expression. What particularly stands out for me in this regard is the contrast between the styles of a Pat Cummings and a Sheila Hamanaka, for example. I find the differences in their styles and the responses to their work very enlivening and very exciting. Pat's art is open and outgoing, while Sheila's is more intensely political. In a way, Sheila's art is confrontational, but this in no way limits her own vision. Pat Cummings, on the other hand, presents us with symbols that immediately draw us in, because they are so familiar. They are so with us. The differences between Pat and Sheila stylistically are not unlike the differences between writers like Ernest Hemingway and William Faulkner. Both of these writers have amazing styles, as do Pat and Sheila, and like Pat and Sheila, both are remarkably different from one another. Hemingway's simplicity eases you into the work, whereas Faulkner's complexity makes the entry difficult. The illustrators who participate in the Conference reveal a similar range of styles, temperaments, and subject matter. And given its cultural theme, the Conference showcases the wide-ranging ethnicity that now characterizes the world of books for young people. This is particularly important for illustrators of parallel cultures who have to struggle to build a constituency.

M/B: They have to do this even now when publishers are so much more willing than they were in the past to acknowledge the parallel cultures that make up this country?

VH: Even now, because these artists are a minority in a huge country, and like all people of parallel culture, they have to work harder at proving themselves than do their colleagues from the dominant culture. This is a very good time for African American and ethnic illustrators. What they must do is to be consistent in their artistry and not get waylaid by commercialism. They need to remain true to their art and genuine about the cultural experiences they're depicting. That's the challenge for all of us working as artists in a multicultural world. If we do these things, we will draw people to our work by the sheer force of our commitment.

VIRGINIA HAMILTON'S ILLUSTRATORS

Zeely. Illustrated by Symeon Shimin. New York: Macmillan, 1967.

The House of Dies Drear. Illustrated by Eros Keith. New York: Macmillan, 1968.

The Time-Ago Tales of Jahdu. Illustrated by Nonny Hogrogian. New York: Macmillan, 1969.

Time-Ago Lost: More Tales of Jahdu. Illustrated by Ray Prather. New York: Macmillan, 1973.

Jahdu. Illustrated by Jerry Pinkney. New York: Greenwillow, 1980.

The People Could Fly: American Black Folktales. Illustrated by Leo and Diane Dillon. New York: Knopf, 1985.

In the Beginning: Creation Stories from Around the World. Illustrated by Barry Moser. San Diego, CA: Harcourt, 1988.

The Bells of Christmas. Illustrated by Lambert Davis. San Diego, CA: Harcourt, 1989.

The Dark Way: Stories from the Spirit World. Illustrated by Barry Moser. San Diego, CA: Harcourt, 1990.

The All Jahdu Storybook. Illustrated by Barry Moser. San Diego, CA: Harcourt, 1991.

Drylongso. Illustrated by Jerry Pinkney. San Diego, CA: Harcourt, 1992.

Many Thousand Gone: African Americans from Slavery to Freedom. Illustrated by Leo and Diane Dillon. New York: Knopf, 1992.

Her Stories: African American Folktales, Fairy Tales, and True Tales. Illustrated by Leo and Diane Dillon. New York: Blue Sky, 1995.

Jaguarundi. Illustrated by Floyd Cooper. New York: Blue Sky, 1995.

When Birds Could Talk & Bats Could Sing. Illustrated by Barry Moser. New York: Blue Sky, 1996.

ABOUT THE AUTHORS

Anthony L. Manna and Carolyn S. Brodie are co-directors of the Virginia Hamilton Conference and co-editors of *Many Faces, Many Voices: Multicultural Literary Experiences for Youth* (Highsmith Press, 1992), a collection of proceedings from the Virginia Hamilton Conference.

Dear Ms. Back Row:

I think
I like you
a lot, especially
since
Christmas
when you wore that angel
crown on top of your so
f l u f f y b r o w n h a i r.
Just
smile
at me
o n e
time
on your way past my desk.

Yours: First Seat First Row.

"Dear Ms. Back Row:" from *Love Letters* by Arnold Adoff, illustrated by Lisa Desimini.

BOOKS BY ARNOLD ADOFF

Illustrated Poetry Books

Black is brown is tan. Illustrated by Emily Arnold McCully. New York: HarperCollins, 1973.

Eats: Poems. Illustrated by Susan Russo. New York: Lothrop, 1979.

Birds. Illustrated by Troy Howell. New York: HarperCollins, 1982

All the Colors of the Race. Illustrated by John Steptoe. New York: Lothrop, 1982.

Sports Pages. Illustrated by Steve Kuzma. New York: HarperCollins, 1986.

The Cabbages Are Chasing the Rabbits. Illustrated by Janet Stevens. New York: Harcourt, 1988.

Chocolate Dreams. Illustrated by Turi MacCombie. New York: Lothrop, 1988.

Greens: Poems. Illustrated by Betsy Lewin. New York: Lothrop, 1988.

In for Winter, Out for Spring. Illustrated by Jerry Pinkney. New York: Harcourt, 1991.

Street Music: City Poems. Illustrated by Karen Barbour. New York: HarperCollins, 1996.

Slow Dance Heart Break Blues. Illustrated by William Cotton. New York: Lothrop, 1996.

Love Letters. Illustrated by Lisa Desimini. Dallas, TX: Blue Sky, 1997.

Poetry Anthologies

I Am the Darker Brother: An Anthology of Modern Poems by Negro Americans. New York: Macmillan, 1968.

The Poetry of Black America. New York: HarperCollins, 1973.

My Black Me: A Beginning Book of Black Poetry. New York: Dutton, 1974.

Prose Anthology and Poet's Prose

Flamboyan. Illustrated by Karen Barbour. New York: Harcourt, 1988.

Hard to be Six. Illustrated by Cheryl Hanna. New York: Lothrop, 1991.

Biography

Malcolm X. Illustrated by John Wilson. New York: HarperCollins, 1970.

ABOUT ARNOLD ADOFF

With the publication of *I Am the Darker Brother: An Anthology of Modern Poems by Negro Americans* in 1963, Arnold Adoff launched a distinguished career as a poet and anthologist. Over the years, he has published more than thirty books for young readers and their "older allies." Illustrated collections of his own poems include *Black is brown is tan*, a *School Library Journal* Best Book, *Eats: Poems*, an American Library Association Notable Children's Book and a *Booklist* Children's Editors' Choice, *All the Colors of the Race*, recipient of the Jane Addams Children's Book Award and a Reading Rainbow Book, *Sports Pages*, a National Council of Teachers of English Teachers' Choice and a Reading Rainbow Featured Selection, *Street Music: City Poems*, an Association for Library Service to Children Notable Book, and *Slow Dance Heart Break Blues*, a *School Library Journal* Best Book for Young Adults. He also has compiled two other groundbreaking anthologies: *My Black Me: A Beginning Book of Black Poetry* and *The Poetry of Black America*.

Arnold Adoff was awarded the 1988 National Council of Teachers of English Award for Excellence in Poetry for Children and for the body of his work.

Illustration by Jerry Pinkney.

2

THE WRINKLE OF SKIN, THE FOLD OF CLOTH
CONVERSATIONS WITH JERRY PINKNEY

DARWIN L. HENDERSON AND ANTHONY L. MANNA

OUR CONVERSATIONS WITH Jerry Pinkney began in the mid 1980s when we set out to learn how an accomplished illustrator constructs picture books, particularly books which explore cultural experiences. In those early discussions, Mr. Pinkney virtually welcomed us into his studio to give us a firsthand account of the dynamic process that consumes him whenever he brings a manuscript to its picture book form. The more we talked with him, the more we came to respect the amazing insight and remarkable skill he brings to the art of the illustrated book. As we wrote in an earlier article about his process, "Pinkney pursues a text the way an actor explores a play script. He searches for clues which signal the texture, shape, and movement of character in action in order to give these elements visual life and to endow them with a distinctive style."[1] We soon learned that, for Jerry Pinkney, the page literally becomes a stage. Like a director, he discovers the focus for a book by using models—himself, family members, friends, children—who dress in costumes for each role and improvise sections of the text. This, he told us, is how he has learned to reconcile the demands of the continuity of the picture book form to his own vision of it, so that, in turn, his audience can "move around the space where the story takes place and explore."[2]

With the same gracious and informative style that colored our early conversations, Jerry Pinkney won over his audience at the 1990 Virginia Hamilton Conference. In his enlightening keynote address, he used slides to chronicle the history of his development as an artist and to explore his ongoing commitment to depicting the experiences of the parallel cultures that continue to shape this country. He gave his audience an insider's view of his vision and art as he laid out the route he has taken from an early career in graphic design to his current full-time concentration on picture book illustration. As he documented his career over the course of more than 30 illustrated books, he drew attention to a sure and steady progression from stunning, spare line drawings to a rich, eclectic palette, from abbreviated suggestions of character and incident to fully orchestrated picture book texts, and from simple staging of the page to greater experimentation with the dramatic textures of the situations found in the texts he has illustrated.

At the conference, Jerry Pinkney revealed another side of his personality—his wonderful sense of humor. At times he kept his audience in stitches with stories about the everyday life of an illustrator. He told, for example, about models who won't cooperate and therefore complicate the whole process of making early sketches. Included among these uncooperative models is his own granddaughter, who, when it came time to act out the role of the robin in *Pretend You're a Cat*, insisted on being a rabbit. To solve this problem, Mr. Pinkney had his granddaughter pose in a ballerina costume and invited the ballerina to assume the posture and attitude of the robin. And he also won his audience over, to much applause, when he revealed that he actually reads the manuscripts for both the novels and picture books he is asked to illustrate. This, he said, is surely one of the chief ironies in his life, considering he initially went into art in order to avoid reading.

Virginia Hamilton has called Jerry Pinkney "one of the finest illustrators of our time." And his critics agree. He is a three-time Caldecott Honor Medalist and the only artist ever to have won three Coretta Scott King Awards for illustration. In addition, he holds three Gold Medals from the Society of Illustrators and two *New York Times* Best Illustrated Book Awards. His illustrations for Julius Lester's retelling of *John Henry* won the *Boston Globe-Horn Book* Award. *John Henry* also received the American Folklore Society's 1994 Aesop Prize for writing and illustration.

In this interview we bring together a number of our phone conversations with Jerry Pinkney and highlights from his address at the sixth annual Virginia Hamilton Conference.

H/M: Jerry, we want to thank you for taking time to talk with us. First off, did you always want to be an artist?

JP: As a child I always drew, and I can truly say that I've always loved the act of drawing. I think drawing was a way of creating my own space. I grew up in a small house in a large family. So drawing became a way of finding my own place to be. My drawing pad became my own room when I didn't have a room of my own. I also think I turned to drawing because I was having problems expressing myself in other ways, but it wasn't until much later that the idea of actually making art for a living came in.

H/M: When you did set out to be an artist, did you intend to be a children's book illustrator?

JP: No, I started off in commercial art courses at Dobbins Vocational High School in Philadelphia. In the beginning I thought I would use my talent to solve problems in the applied arts, advertising and design, not in illustration or the fine arts. When I left Dobbins, it was suggested that it wouldn't be possible to make a living as an African American artist in painting or illustration. I then applied for and received a scholarship to the Philadelphia Museum College of Art, where I majored in advertising and design. But later I realized that my real passion was for drawing and painting. After I completed art school, I settled in Boston and discovered the publishing community there. That's when I became intrigued by the idea of making books that combined my interests.

H/M: Which interests?

JP: What I found in book illustration was a terrific marriage of the disciplines of drawing, painting, and design. I discovered that words and pictures could go together in a compelling way, and that's how I arrived at an interest in books. For me it started with collecting books and being fascinated with the idea that books are something physical, something you can hold and savor. I was equally fascinated by typography, and I still think that when you talk about typography, you're also talking about good drawing. And then, of course, you have illustration, you have the art.

H/M: How do you envision your responsibility to a text, particularly to its language?

JP: For me, interpretation of the text is foremost in my mind. My responsibility is to be true to the text and at the same time to find my own vehicle for expressing the ideas I discover in it. What I'm doing, I believe, is paralleling the text without mimicking it. I need to find my own voice and tell the story from that vantage point.

H/M: In your presentation at the Virginia Hamilton Conference you said that a text is a way for you to travel. What do you mean by that?

JP: From an early age, I looked at pictures as a vehicle for introducing me to different places, faraway lands, and people much different from myself. I remember trying to put myself in those other places and wondering how people in a particular culture might think or feel and what rituals they may have practiced that were different from those of my own culture. You'll notice that some of the books I've illustrated over the years take place outside my own culture. I use books as the means to travel to and understand other places and other cultures.

H/M: What kinds of texts are you especially interested in illustrating? Which texts give you the most pleasure?

JP: I love to do period pieces, and I also love to do fantasy. I did a number of projects back to back which dealt with plantation life. One was a large project for the Booker T. Washington National Monument in Rocky Mountain, Virginia. Through that research I went on to illustrate *Minty: A Story of Young Harriet Tubman*. Then I had the opportunity to work on a new telling of *Little Black Sambo—Sam and the Tigers*—which is total fantasy. When I was doing the period pieces I thought to myself, "This is what I want to do." Then when I finished them, I realized that there was something I hadn't done that I very much wanted to do. So Julius Lester and I developed the idea for *Sam and the Tigers,* and Julius wrote an extraordinary text. Now I'm moving out of period projects for a while to projects that are more fanciful. I will try to follow that up with another piece that deals with history. Moving between projects like these allows me to keep a sense of freshness in my work.

H/M: Here's a question from a university student who has studied your work and introduced your books to her students in the sixth grade. She asks, "Does Jerry Pinkney have to be touched by a book in order to illustrate it?"

JP: I'm fortunate to be in a position where I can seek out manuscripts that genuinely interest me at a given time. Being moved is very important to me. There are many reasons why a particular story may touch me. In the case of the "Uncle Remus" tales, it had a lot to do with stories I had heard growing up. They were part of my growing up years. In the case of *Minty*, I was certainly moved by Alan Schroeder's manuscript which dealt with the life of the young Harriet Tubman. I have a lot of respect for her life and her spirit and her courage. So each book brings to it its own electricity, and I usually feel some of that in my first reading.

H/M: When you first face the plain white space that's going to become the pictured text, what do you imagine?

JP: First of all, I read the text to become thoroughly familiar with it. The text will usually tell me what it needs. I then have to determine how best to craft that need or idea. Often, there's a part of the text that has more of a *need* to be illustrated than a part that I might *want* to illustrate. I have an obligation to respond to the call of the text. Once those decisions are made, I begin the process of illustrating by preparing thumbnail sketches. But where I focus always stems from what the text tells me I should do.

H/M: How do you know which incidents or characters to illustrate?

JP: It's a feeling. I will sometimes think, "This passage would make a great illustration." But another voice will respond, "Yes it could make a great illustration, but how much will it add to the text?" I think what I'm trying to say here is that I always need to be conscious of whether I'm illustrating for myself or because the story, the text, demands it. And oftentimes I will abandon an illustration I really want to do for the sake of illustrating what the text calls for. It's a real balancing act.

H/M: How, for example, did you find the concept for *Mirandy and Brother Wind*?

JP: *Mirandy* allowed me to speak to some aspects of African American culture that have become important to me. The book became a platform for me to address the culture. I set out to focus as authentically as possible on small, significant details such as the fabric Miss Poinsettia and Mirandy are wearing, the style of the houses, the types of flowers that surround the houses, and so forth. I also wanted to speak to African Americans about the importance of going to church for the cake walk. The text provided the springboard to address those things, and it allowed me enough space to do this adequately. All those elements became part of my vision for this book.

H/M: How did your concept for *Drylongso* evolve?

JP: I'm glad you brought that book up. I think of it as one of my most successful in terms of interpreting a text. Virginia Hamilton is an amazing writer, but a challenging read. She gave me a tremendous degree of freedom because *Drylongso* is very mythical and yet realistic at the same time. My responsibility to *Drylongso* was to bring a certain degree of tension to the illustrations. Most of the story deals with characters talking and relating to each other. My role was to work with the space, the house where the story takes place, and to breathe into that one room a sense of magic and tension.

H/M: Do you usually collaborate with the writers whose texts you're illustrating?

JP: In most cases, yes. When I work with Julius Lester, for instance, the text is sent to me and then we talk about my concept for the book.

A good example of this is how we went about the process for *John Henry*. It was a project I had wanted to do for some time, and Phyllis Fogelman, my editor at Dial, and I approached Julius to see if he was interested. After several conversations, Julius and I came to a mutual direction and vision for the book.

H/M: What was that vision?

JP: We both wanted people to relate to John Henry as a man. Although he will always be thought of as heroic and very strong and powerful, the John Henry we were after is also a flesh-and-blood human being.

H/M: People often wonder about the process a book undergoes once the illustrations are submitted. It seems that an illustrated book passes through many hands before it hits the market. Would you talk about that process?

JP: Well, the process has a lot to do with my other discipline, which is book design. I never could separate illustration and design. I'm interested in the entire creation of the book. Many artists are not. Fortunately, I'm involved in every aspect of production, with the exception of the paper. I review the proofs with the art director and the production staff, and the book doesn't go to press until I approve the proofs. I'm also involved in promoting the book through the marketing department. I even worked with the designer at Dial to come up with the poster for *Minty*. The publishing houses I work with have come to understand that I'm going to be present at each and every turn a book of mine takes.

H/M: In your acceptance speech for the *Boston Globe-Horn Book* Award for *John Henry*, you acknowledge Atha Tehon at Dial for "outstanding art direction." What role does an art director have, and how is this role different from yours?

JP: For me, an art director is someone to bounce visual ideas off of, someone to whom I can say, "Could we look at this another way?" or someone to push me toward closure. It's through this dialogue that I can move my ideas along. In a way, then, one side of me is saying that I do have a tremendous amount of control over a book, while the other side is saying that it's important to work with an art director you respect and trust in order to make a stronger book. I've worked with Atha Tehon for many years, so we've developed a mutual trust. And Atha, in turn, works with a designer named Jane Bierhorst. I always request Jane now, because her sense of design and typography complements my work. It's an interesting thing to have control.

Maybe having control is knowing when to ask for help.

H/M: Another student has a question for you. She asks, "Your visual images are so powerful. How do prevent these images from overpowering the text? How do you achieve balance?"

JP: Each book presents its own challenge. For instance, with *John Henry*, where the spirit and strength of the character are so powerful, the artwork had to feel large, as if John Henry were too large for the pages of the book to hold. In designing the book, it was decided that to get that power across, we should keep the illustrations separate from the text. With *The Talking Eggs* it seemed that the best way to achieve balance and harmony was to have the illustrations move gently around the text. In illustration, the goal is to make the art be one with the text, so that the audience feels that neither the art nor the text is more important than the other. There also are times when I feel the function of my illustrations is to gently complement the text, as in *Back Home* by Gloria Jean Pinkney. That's all part of the vision for each book.

H/M: Here's a question that goes off in a different direction. When we're reading your books, we can't help but notice what a warm feeling you have for animal characters. How did that evolve?

JP: *Turtle in July* is one of my favorite books to talk about when the topic of animals comes up. The book is basically a series of portraits of animals, with the bullhead character being the thread that holds the whole thing together. I was trying to respond to the poems, but I also wanted to reach into the inner life of the animals. With the "Uncle Remus" stories, I entered the illustration process with a great deal of respect for the creatures. I wanted to make them believable in a kind of humorous, human way.

H/M: As we're talking with you, we've spread many of your books across a table. From this vantage point, it becomes apparent that in each of the books we're seeing what might best be described as the wrinkle of skin and the fold of cloth. It's as though we're observing many of the wrinkles and folds of life.

JP: If illustration is true creative work, then you're speaking about life. You're speaking about what you sense and how you feel about things. I want to see life in its best way. I want to see it glowing. I think that what I'm trying to do in my work is to give everything a sense of life, a feeling of positive light. And yet I don't want to romanticize life. The way to avoid this, I believe, is to individualize every thing and every person I paint.

H/M: In your presentation at the Virginia Hamilton Conference, you compared shaping an illustration with staging a scene. What do you mean by that?

JP: I see my illustrations as theatre, and, as in the theatre, there's a depth I want my viewer to walk into when moving through a book I've illustrated. I want it to seem that if somebody leans too far over when reading my books, he or she may fall into the space. So the staging is that of theatre, with a strong sense of what theatre does, which is to require you to enter and participate. Staging the page becomes very important in creating a space that the viewer feels compelled to enter.

H/M: You've often talked about how you use models in your work. Why do you do this?

JP: The reason for working with models is to maintain a character's continuity throughout the book. After all, you want the viewer to recognize the characters and to get to know them as the situation in the book moves along. Now the choice of models and how I work with them is another thing altogether. My wife Gloria has been incredibly helpful when it comes to finding models. What I'll do is come up with some drawings, and Gloria and I will talk about how a character should look and feel. Sometimes we look for a model with a certain personality, because we want a particular fit between the model and the character. As you can tell, for me it's much more involved than simply bringing models into the studio and directing them. There has to be an exchange with the models in order to get them to respond, and that response is not only to me, but to the text so that they begin to suggest things about the character and the situation. When I did *I Want to Be*, we went to playgrounds with the young girl who modeled, and we met her in her home. We read the poem together and asked her to respond to it; first in ways we suggested, but later in letting her have a go at it. We followed her around the playground and took photographs of her doing things and later related the photos to the poem. So using models is a very complicated process because it has a lot to do with an intuitiveness about what the text needs.

H/M: In which books do you think your use of models has been particularly rewarding?

JP: The model for the character of John Henry was a fascinating man. He brought so much to that book because of his interest in the story and his willingness to participate in the entire process of realizing our vision for the book. In the case of *Back Home* and *The Sunday Outing*, books which my wife Gloria wrote about experiences from her youth, the young girl Gloria found to do the modeling didn't look like Gloria looked when she was young, but she did have a similar personality. That's important, because the closer the temperament of the model is to the character I have in mind, the easier it is for the model to become the character. So you see, the purpose of using models is to help me create the characters. When I sit down to draw, I'm not actually working from a photograph; I'm drawing on the experience I had with the model.

H/M: You've often served as your own model. In which books did you do that?

JP: Early on I posed for most of the figures in *Tonweya and the Eagles*, which is a collection of traditional Lakota tales. I even posed for the figure of the Indian maiden in that book; she's the one with her back to the reader. I also was the model for many of the background characters in *John Henry* and for nearly every character in *The Man Who Kept His Heart in a Bucket*. As far as modeling goes, *The Man Who Kept His Heart in a Bucket* was an interesting book to work with. I would mark a spot in the text and become one of the characters doing something there. Then I would mark another passage and be the character who's responding to the character I portrayed in the earlier passage. I had to look through many books to be sure that the portraits I was coming up with looked accurate, historically speaking, that is. You can also find me in *Mirandy and Brother Wind*, where I was the model for the Brother Wind character.

H/M: We understand that there's an interesting story behind your use of models for the "Uncle Remus" books. You started with a different concept than the one we see in the these books.

JP: I started working on those stories with pictorial references of the animals, but I ran into difficulty because I couldn't express what I was after by using pictures. I thought that the animals weren't becoming as anthropomorphic as I wanted them to be. So, after a number of sketches, I simply posed for the animals myself. Gloria and I went to the local Goodwill and bought some baggy pants, a vest, and some shirts, which we felt reflected the period of the stories. I then posed to suggest both animal and human at the same time. It became an interesting concept to work with, and it was a lot of fun. I'm fascinated by other times, by the clothing and other details of other times, but also by the attitudes that prevailed.

H/M: What kind of research do you usually do when you're working on a period piece?

JP: I start off by trying to center on a particular place and time. Right now I'm working on a book that takes place in Virginia, but not in a particular time period. In the book there's a logging company that uses water for power, which means that I need to contact a research house for everything they can find on the history of water-powered sawmills. Then I'll augment what they come up with by going to a library system in a particular region of Virginia to get more help.

H/M: Is your research always as extensive as this?

JP: It's very extensive and the detailing is unbelievable. With *Minty*, for example, I worked with the National Park Service in Harper's Ferry, West Virginia, which aided me even with the simplest of details. For instance, I needed to know what the slaveholders drank with their evening meals. Other writers suggested that there would be a pitcher of milk on the table, but that didn't sound right to me. When I informed the people at the National Park Service that *Minty* was set in Virginia in the 1840s, they told me that people back then would be drinking cider or beer with their meals. There are so many little specific things like that, which you have to know in order to make the pictures accurate. In *John Henry*, the main thing was clothing. And not only the style of the clothing, but the cloth itself and the colors of the time. When I researched the colors of the period in which we set the book, I found that most clothing had a touch of gray to it, with the exception of indigo blue and red, which were brilliant. But in general, the clothing of the period was drab; it took a lot of money to import something very bright. I learned that red and yellow dyes were developed during those times, and red was particularly expensive to manufacture. And on and on it goes.

H/M: Jerry, what do you want children to get from the books you illustrate?

JP: First, I want people to enjoy what I do. I want them to look, to see deeply, and this, of course, comes from a person who deals in visual images. I want people of all ages to see that there's something magical about the way I've rendered the subject matter. And if they look at a picture of mine and say it's great, I'm satisfied.

H/M: One of the recurring themes in your work is the child-as-hero. Why is this important to you?

JP: I wonder if those heroes help me with my own life.

H/M: And do they?

JP: I think so.

H/M: How?

JP: Because they are always courageous. I think of courage as an important quality of the human spirit; it's what makes a person stand up for something important. I think that people who look for their own voice and their own way of living have to be courageous. When I look at the last few books I've done—*I Want to Be, John Henry, Minty, Sam and the Tigers*—I see a long line of heroes. With *Sam and the Tigers* I take an image of a character that symbolizes an enormous stereotype and transform it, so that Sam becomes a courageous young man. In Julius's and my version of the story, Sam doesn't accidentally get his clothing back; he does this by outsmarting the tigers as he becomes a hero.

H/M: What do you think your books contribute to cultural understanding?

JP: I like the idea of celebrating people, life, and humanity. That's what I hope comes through my work. I want people to believe that I care, that I love them, that I'm celebrating them. What I've always thought of myself doing is establishing a link among people. And this comes out in the way I go about making books. I am mostly telling the story of African Americans through a realistic style. Because it's realistic, it allows me to individualize and personalize cultural experience. This carries over to how I deal with other cultures as well, especially those cultures which have been denied personalized attention. I want people to see the value of my own culture, but in order to do that I have to value other cultures, which is to say that there is a connection among all human beings. Because I'm a curious person, I'm interested in the similarities and differences among people. As an artist, I think it's my responsibility to share this interest. The research I do certainly helps me here because it offers me references to draw on, and I'm not only talking about visual references; I'm talking about references to the spirit of the culture I happen to be dealing with at the time. Have I told you about "Building Bridges," the traveling exhibit of my art, which I recently put together? Originally it was to have 40 or 50 pieces on African American culture, but I've expanded that notion to include pieces I've done on Lakota, Central American, and Eastern European life. So you see, it's that business of finding the connections that unite people around the world. Some of the books I've illustrated have been translated into many different languages. When I talk to children about this, I tell them that it shows not only how books travel to other cultures, but also how we can travel to other cultures through books.

H/M: What do you consider your greatest accomplishment?

JP: I guess having a dream come true.

H/M: What is that dream?

JP: Having the patience to let things unfold. It took a long time for me to get to this place in my career, but I stayed with the dream that some day I would be free enough and good enough to be in a place where I could express my ideas through art.

H/M: And we think that has a whole lot to do with the sincerity of your vision.

Notes

1. Darwin L. Henderson and Anthony L. Manna. "An Interview With Jerry Pinkney," *Children's Literature in Education*, 21.3, 1990, p. 135.

2. Jerry Pinkney. "The Artist at Work: Characters Interacting With the Viewer," *The Horn Book Magazine*, 67.2, 1991, p. 174.

SELECTED BOOKS ILLUSTRATED BY JERRY PINKNEY

The Adventures of Spider. Written by Joyce Arkhurst. Boston: Little, Brown, 1964.

Femi and Old Grandaddie. Written by Adjai Robinson. New York: Coward, 1971.

Song of the Trees. Written by Mildred D. Taylor. New York: Dial, 1975.

Yagua Days. Written by Cruz Martel. New York: Dial, 1976.

Mary McLeod Bethune. Written by Eloise Greenfield. New York: Harper, 1977.

Tonweya and the Eagles and Other Lakota Indian Tales. Written by Rosebud Yellow Robe. New York: Dial, 1979.

Jahdu. Written by Virginia Hamilton. New York: Greenwillow, 1980.

The Patchwork Quilt. Written by Valerie Flournoy. New York: Dial, 1985.

The Tales of Uncle Remus. Written by Julius Lester. New York: Dial, 1987.

More Tales of Uncle Remus. Written by Julius Lester. New York: Dial, 1988.

Mirandy and Brother Wind. Written by Patricia McKissack. New York: Knopf, 1988.

The Talking Eggs. Written by Robert D. San Souci. New York: Dial, 1989.

Further Tales of Uncle Remus. Written by Julius Lester. New York: Dial, 1990.

Turtle in July. Written by Marilyn Singer. New York: Macmillan, 1989.

Pretend You're a Cat. Written by Jean Marzollo. New York: Dial, 1990.

In for Winter, Out for Spring. Written by Arnold Adoff. New York: Harcourt, 1991.

The Man Who Kept His Heart in a Bucket. Written by Sonia Levitin. New York: Dial, 1991.

Drylongso. Written by Virginia Hamilton. New York: Harcourt, 1992.

Back Home. Written by Gloria Jean Pinkney. New York: Dial, 1992.

I Want to Be. Written by Thylias Moss. New York: Dial, 1993.

A Starlit Somersault Downhill. Written by Nancy Willard. Boston, MA: Little, Brown, 1993.

John Henry. Written by Julius Lester. New York: Dial, 1994.

The Last Tales of Uncle Remus. Written by Julius Lester. New York: Dial, 1994.

The Sunday Outing. Written by Gloria Jean Pinkney. New York: Dial, 1994.

Minty: A Story of Young Harriet Tubman. Written by Alan Schroeder. New York: Dial, 1995.

Sam and the Tigers. Written by Julius Lester. New York: Dial, 1996.

ABOUT THE AUTHORS

Darwin L. Henderson is an associate professor of literacy and children's literature at the University of Cincinnati. Anthony L. Manna, founder and co-director of the Virginia Hamilton Conference, is a professor of drama and children's and young adult literature at Kent State University.

C.L.O.U.D.S. written and illustrated by Pat Cummings.

3

GLOBAL VISUALS

PAT CUMMINGS

THE PALETTE I work with as an illustrator is very wide because children's imaginations cover such a large territory. Children are wonderfully receptive. They're open-minded and always ready to accept new experiences. For an illustrator, it's both a delight and a challenge to reach such fertile imaginations. It means you can fill your books with powerful images and ideas, but it also means that you face a big responsibility. While you can try to keep children's imaginations alive by offering them a lot to think about and visualize, you have to be careful not to strain their belief by overwhelming them. I used to tell my niece a lot of things about the world until she stopped believing me. When I took her to the Metropolitan Museum in New York to see the King Tut exhibit, I informed her that there was a boy king inside King Tut's mummy. She went to her mother and said, "Mom, she's doing it again." She stopped believing me after awhile because I tried too hard to tell her too much. My niece taught me a powerful lesson about how to come across to the kids who read the books I make.

Still, as an artist, I like to draw on the amazing images I've come upon through years of observing and traveling. I was lucky. I grew up, as some folks would say, as an "army brat," which means I moved a lot from culture to culture with my military family. From an early age I was constantly being introduced to all sorts of rich visual experiences. In Germany, we would visit castles and then later read or listen to German fairy tales that would have a similar setting. Those excursions turned fantasy into a very real, imaginable thing for me, because fairy tales were now as tangible as the stairs we would climb to reach a castle on the Rhine. In Okinawa, my American girlfriends and I would often go out to a village where we'd see water buffalo and people who allegedly were witches. There would be reports on the front page of the Okinawa newspaper telling about a ghost that had made another appearance. I remember that mystery and witchcraft were important aspects of this culture, but more in the order of everyday beliefs rather than as occult or weird phenomena. Growing up with experiences like these, I soon developed a respect for various cultures and the riches they hold. I learned not to make light of other cultures, not to pass judgment on them, but to embrace their richness. It's not surprising, then, that certain aspects of the cultures I've experienced and the ones I've only dreamed about work their way into my art in some fashion. It might be a pattern in a fabric I've seen in Guatemala or a design I've picked up in some African country. By putting images and objects from different cultures in my books, I'm making these cultures accessible to kids, more commonplace, less foreign. Familiarity with other cultures, I believe, can bring about an understanding of other cultures, and respect is not such a great distance from understanding. It's too easy to have a narrow focus if you are born and bred in one small area of the world. You need to force yourself to look outside your own city, your own town, your own neighborhood, to take in other cultures. Good books can help you do this.

When I'm doing illustrations for books, I tend to show black people. As I travel around the country visiting schools, I've had teachers and librarians tell me that my books aren't available in their schools because they don't have a black population. These same folks usually have a copy of C.L.O.U.D.S., though, which I've done with a cast of blue characters. Do they have blue kids in their schools? My point is that although my books feature African Americans, the topics tend to be ones that all kids are concerned about. In my travels, I rarely meet kids who ask me why my books contain black children—or blue, for that matter—or if the story is only for African Americans. I've never had a child come to me and say, "This is a black story, isn't it?"

No, it's a story about coping with sibling rivalry, or surviving the first day at school, or finding a new lunch box, and it just happens that the kids and families are black. That's one side of the story. The other side is that, yes, in the books I both write and illustrate, as well as in the ones I illustrate for other writers, I'm glad to be casting the experience in an African American mode. After all, I want to make sure that books with African American characters are available to children of every hue and background. I clearly remember when they weren't.

People often ask me how I got started in the publishing business. I started out doing illustrations for theatres, newspapers, and magazines. Then I did what you call "schlepping" your way to book publishers. You go up and down the avenue with your portfolio and visit as many publishing houses as you can. It takes a while to make a contact that leads to anything substantial. Along the way, you meet art directors and editors who might say, "Your portfolio is filled with frogs; we're looking for turtles," so you have to keep at it.

While I was schlepping my way around New York City, I happened upon the Council on Interracial Books for Children. This organization often featured photographers and illustrators in their newsletter. After they featured some of my work, an editor contacted me to ask if I'd like to illustrate a book for her company. Would I like to? I tried to appear nonchalant and very professional about the offer—as though I'd been illustrating books for years—but I literally ran to her office. "Do you know how to do a book?" was what she asked me. She wanted me to come up with the complete design for the book, from the colors to the size.

Well, I had been involved in a lot of commercial freelancing for awhile, so this business of doing a book shouldn't be a problem, right? But once I sat down with the manuscript, which was Eloise Greenfield's text for *Good News*, I realized I didn't have a clue about how to proceed. Fortunately, through a friend of a friend, I was able to locate illustrator Tom Feelings, who, as it turned out, was very generous with his time and talent. He led me through the entire process of putting a book together, and he also calmed me down, because I was convinced that the illustrations for this book should rival Tenniel's for *Alice in Wonderland*. I wanted to include everything I knew and, so it seemed, every technique I had a grasp of. Luckily, Tom Feelings discouraged me from doing this. I owe that man quite a professional debt, the moral of the story being that it's important to help beginning artists as Tom helped me.

Since that first book in 1977, I've gone on to illustrate more than a dozen books for others, and I've done a few of my own. *Just Us Women* is one of the early books I illustrated. Jeannette Caines wrote the story about her family, but I used people in my own family as models. In the story, a young girl and her favorite aunt are getting ready for a trip to North Carolina in the aunt's new car. These two are quite a pair. I like working with strong and assertive characters like these, and I especially like young kids with chutzpah, with some self-assurance. So, in the illustration where I show the niece looking at a statue of an eagle, I imagined her matching the statue's fierceness with a fierce look of her own. That's the kind of kid I wanted her to be.

As they plan their trip, they imagine what they'll see and do on their excursion, what they'll eat, the junk they'll buy, and generally how they'll break away from the routines they're used to. For an illustrator, a trip like this one is a great opportunity to do some detailed work, and to put all sorts of personally meaningful things in the pictures. For example, when Aunt Martha and her niece stop at a road-side market, the stuff I have them looking through includes two bookends with Dutch figures that are staring at one another. My mother had those bookends on her shelf forever, and I drew them into the picture because they had always fascinated me when I was growing up. Those bookends just popped into my mind when I was working on that illustration. There's also a full-page spread of Aunt Martha and her niece packing some maps. To do this page, I picked up a map at a local gas station, made a copy, and did some cutting and pasting to get the map into the picture. My editor wondered how long it must have taken me to get such a detailed map on the page. "It was nothing," I said.

When I was working on *Just Us Women*, I would often meet with the art director at what is now called HarperCollins. One day he told me that the woman in the office I was passing by on the way to his office was Jeannette Caines. I remember he told me that I shouldn't let the editors know that I knew this. A lot of the time, editors discourage writers and illustrators from contacting each other. When I was new to the publishing field, I couldn't understand this, but now that I've written a few books of my own, I can appreciate the policy. I now realize that there are some authors who will tell you right down to every minute detail what an illustration should look like. It's only natural that they would. After all, since they created the story and the characters, they have a very clear picture in their mind of how and where the story takes place, and of how the characters look and act. How hard it would be to draw exactly what's in their minds, rather than in my own imagination. No wonder editors tend to keep author and illustrator separated.

In *My Mama Needs Me*, Mildred Pitts Walter tells the story of a little boy whose mother comes home from the hospital with a brand new baby. I fell in love with this story from the very beginning because it hit home. According to stories I've heard in my own family, when my mother came home with my new sister, Barbara, my brother Artie couldn't walk past her crib without taking a swipe at her. Knowing this, I really felt obligated to do the manuscript justice. So I read it over and over again before I found the right pitch. What I think Mildred Pitts Walter did so beautifully was to break down sibling rivalry into authentic and therefore believable emotions. "Sibling rivalry" sounds so cold and distant, but in this story it comes fully alive through the interactions among family members and particularly because of Jason's mixed-up feelings. He's very excited about the arrival of the baby, and he definitely wants to participate, though he doesn't know exactly what it all means. Of course, when the baby comes home, she receives a lot of attention, and, naturally, Jason becomes jealous and hurt. This book was a challenge for me, because I wanted to show the wide range of emotions the characters feel as they learn to cope and adjust. Incidentally, the kimono I have the mother wearing is one my friend brought me from Japan. I'm glad I put it in the book, because it fell to shreds and I no longer have it. Illustrations are a way of saving things, and, as *My Mama Needs Me* demonstrates, peoples' feelings certainly count among some of the best things illustrations can preserve.

Fred's First Day was the first book I got to do in full color. In all the other books I had done up to that point, the colors needed to be pre-separated. What this means is that you have to paint every page as many times as it takes to accommodate the number of colors you're using. With *My Mama Needs Me*, for example, I painted each page four times in order to match the four-color printing process that was used. After doing each page four times, I was very happy to work in full color with *Fred's First Day*. Cathy Warren's story is about a middle child facing the difficulties of going to school for the first time. On one page I used cool lavenders and yellows. I remember, though, that when I took it to my editor, she absolutely hated the colors. I was taken aback, to say the least, especially because she had never been that negative about my work before. She called in a group of other editors and art directors to tell them how horrible she felt this combination of colors truly was. After the book was finished, she confided that when she was in high school, the young man she had gone to an Easter dance with had run off with a girl who was wearing a lavender and yellow dress. I should have known!

Storm in the Night, another book I did for Harper, was great fun to illustrate, once I got over the anxiety of trying a new medium. My editor at Harper likes me to try new things. He told me that when he was reading Mary Stolz's manuscript for the book, he immediately envisioned a dark night that also was very vibrant with color. After hearing this, I worked myself into an awful state, calling a friend at three in the morning and tearing up lots of sheets of paper. A dark night, but a night filled with vibrant colors? After some experimenting, I found that acrylics worked best to convey that sense of a deep darkness that's lit up by occasional flashes of lightning. In the story, a young boy is visiting his grandfather when the lights in the house go off during a dramatic electrical storm. I saw the story as taking place somewhere in the south. Mary Stolz lives in Florida, and I've lived in Georgia. I remembered those summer southern nights when it was still very warm, even though it was raining. On such a night as this, with thunder booming and lightning streaking, Thomas and his grandfather, accompanied by grandfather's ever-present cat, Ringo, eventually wind up on the front porch, where grandfather tells Thomas a story to calm his nerves. I show that it's a story within the story—I show it visually, that is—by placing the grandfather and his grandson in the lower right-hand corner of the illustrations, but just a bit beyond the border of the illustrations, on the pages where the grandfather tells his story. In this way, I discovered, I could allow the grandfather's story about his own youth to take over the page, and I did this because young Thomas has a hard time imagining his grandfather as a young man. I felt that this visual pattern emphasized the cross-generational theme that the author, Mary Stolz, is driving at.

I did the illustrations for *I Need a Lunch Box* after I finished working on *Storm in the Night*. This is a true story. Jeannette Caines, who wrote it, was having lunch once with a friend of hers who said she'd been all over town looking for a lunch box for her son. She had promised him one when he started preschool. Even though he knew he would be attending school half days and would be coming home for lunch, he still wanted to carry this empty lunch box to and from school each day. Jeannette returned from that lunch date, sat down, wrote the story in a flash, and immediately sold it to Harper. Do I need to warn you to be very careful when you talk to authors? For this book, I experimented with rubber stamps. Did you know that there's a newspaper called *Rubber Stamp Madness*? I also found out about rubber stamp clubs and an international rubber stamp society. There are lots of people out there stamping.

I loved working with the text of *I Need a Lunch Box* because so much was left unsaid. There was barely one line of text for every page, and this allowed me free rein with regard to the visuals. But I also took to the fact that this preschooler has dreams. For an illustrator, dreams present a wonderful place to exercise imagination and technique.

Following the "lunch box" book, I worked on Joyce Barrett's manuscript for *Willie's Not the Hugging Kind*. This is a sweet story. Willie's a very sensitive kid who's decided, with a little help from his friend Jo-Jo, that hugging is not cool. He teases his sister about needing to hug her stuffed bear when she goes to bed, but the whole time he's hurting inside, because he recalls how wonderful it felt to be hugged and also sees evidence of hugging wherever he turns. So, what does Willie do? He gets by for a while by hugging inanimate objects—a stop sign, a door, his bath towel, his book, and so on. Well, this can go on for only so long, and so he goes back to hugging people. The thing I love about doing picture books is that I get so many opportunities to play with happy endings. Yes, a problem is presented, and, like Willie's here, it's taken seriously. But usually it's resolved by the end of the book, and this turn of events, I feel, is the responsibility of writers and illustrators who work with books for children. You do present a problem and even a crisis, but you also show possible ways to work it out.

Jimmy Lee Did It is the first book I both wrote and illustrated. After years of hearing teachers say that you should always write about what you know, when I first started writing, which topics did I choose? Really bizarre ones with twisted plots. I'd show these tiring stories to editors, all of them very patient folks, who'd return a manuscript of mine with a "hmmmmm." No comment! I learned to calm down, though. I had about ten manuscripts hidden away somewhere, stuff I'd shown no one. One of the editors I'd worked with as an illustrator, asked if I'd ever considered writing. Well, if she hadn't asked, those manuscripts would still be hiding. One simple but important lesson I've learned about writing is that you have to show it to someone at some point. Despite the fear of being rejected and in light of the criticism, you need to have people read what you've written. Otherwise, you'll never grow as a writer.

Jimmy Lee Did It came out of an experience in my family. When I was growing up, my brother had an imaginary friend he called "Jimmy Lee." Jimmy Lee got blamed for everything bad that happened—just about. I mean, when *anything* went wrong, Jimmy Lee was the one who did it. Artie, my brother, was basically guiltless. If something broke, Artie would say that Jimmy Lee did it. Artie's bedroom is a mess, but Artie's reading comic books? Blame it on Jimmy Lee.

I took the opportunity to put lots of other details about Artie in *Jimmy Lee Did It*. To this day, my brother has thousands of comic books. Once, when we were younger, he thought he was a super hero. He went by the name of "The Crampo Kid." His super power, he told me back then, was that he could put cramps in his toes whenever he wanted to. Of course, I couldn't figure out the value of having that power, but Artie felt that if a shady character ever broke into our house some night and entered his room and tied up his feet, he would put cramps in his own toes. The minute the perpetrator escaped from the house, Artie would be able to release the ropes just by willing the cramps out of his feet. I couldn't resist putting a brief escapade from the Crampo Kid, in comic book format, of course, in this book.

The fun part of doing this book was planting clues about the real culprit. For example, that's definitely Artie's foot running off in the picture where "Jimmy Lee" drew pictures on his bedroom wall with crayon. And those are definitely Artie's handprints on the endpapers. Still, when I go into schools with this book, younger children will always ask me who really caused all the problems. Was it the dog? Was it the bear? I've even received some angry letters from kids who can't solve the mystery. Of course, I refuse to tell them who Jimmy Lee is.

The irony of *Jimmy Lee Did It* is that I have the character of Angel, who's actually my sister, attempting to catch Jimmy Lee. In truth, my sister was not at all disturbed by the presence of this invisible character. In fact, she once told me that she and my brother had invented another imaginary person they called "The Captain." But in the book where I'm the one in control, it was my right to decide that Angel should get fed up with Jimmy Lee's pranks and set out to find him by setting a trap. So I have her put out doughnuts and a glass of milk before she takes a nap. While she's sleeping, a hand reaches for a doughnut. Whose could it be? The dog sees, the stuffed bear sees, the eyes in the photograph on the wall see. That illustration of a photograph, by the way, is of my father. Of course, I never tell my family I'm putting them in my books beforehand. I never told Artie I was going to revive the Crampo Kid. When he finally saw the book, my brother told me I had better get a lawyer.

C.L.O.U.D.S. is another book I both wrote and illustrated. It's total fantasy. The concept for the book took shape on my mother's porch in Virginia while we were admiring a particularly amazing sunset. I started playing with the notion that some truly sensitive artist had to be behind such a glorious natural wonder as this sunset surely was. When I wrote the book, I named the artist Chuku. That's my husband's name. It's a Nigerian Ibo name, the longer version of which—Chukemeka—means "God's gift to the family." In Nigeria, it's a name reserved for the firstborn son. My husband uses only the Chuku part, which means "God." Occasionally, I come across people in my audiences who understand the language and sort of gasp when I read the name from the book.

In *C.L.O.U.D.S.*, Chuku is an artist who has just started to work as a cloud designer for the Department of Creative Lights, Opticals, and Unusual Designs in the Sky. But you can imagine his disappointment when he is assigned to work in New York City, where, to Chuku, it seems almost impossible even to see the sky because of all the tall buildings and the dirty air. Why should anybody pay attention to the sky in a place like this? You also can imagine how relieved Chuku is when he finds the inspiration to make the New York City sky as beautiful as any other. At one point, I show Chuku looking down on Central Park, and there he sees a little girl staring intently at the sky. Well, he's inspired now, and off he goes to his office to do a sequence of clouds that will get this child to wonder about the beauty of the skies. When Chuku gets carried away and sends a message to the little girl who is always watching, he gets reprimanded by his boss for breaking one of the cardinal rules of the department. Instead of being relocated to a new and better region because of his other fine work, Chuku will just have to continue overseeing New York's sky, the job nobody wants. Well, this suits Chuku just fine. He's found his niche.

In this book I was working with environmental issues, with an appreciation of the city, and with office politics. The illustrations were easy enough to draw, because I'm familiar with the New York City skyline. From my loft in Brooklyn, I can clearly see the Statue of Liberty. It was such a joy to do these illustrations in full color. I should also mention that the book gave me a lot of satisfaction because I've always loved to do aerial views. Occasionally, I have dreams of flying, and when I was younger, I'd sometimes dream of myself floating over lovely fields and other enticing places. *C.L.O.U.D.S.* gave me an opportunity to recapture the sensations I've experienced in some of my dreams.

When I wrote and illustrated *Clean Your Room, Harvey Moon!*, I decided to change the name of the central character to protect the guilty. This is my brother Artie, once again. My editor wanted to call it "The Day Artie Cummings Cleaned His Room," but nobody I knew wanted to deal with legal fees. Harvey is just about to settle into a Saturday morning of comics and cartoons, when his mother announces that he's got to clean his room. And, as you can see in the illustration I did of his response, Harvey doesn't react well to his mother's demand. He sort of faints. Ask anyone in my family and they'll confirm that the mess I reveal in Harvey's room is a mild version of Artie's. In fact, my father told me that the illustrations wouldn't be accurate unless I included a sock standing up by itself on a bed. When Artie moved out of the house to attend college, there was moss growing on the walls. I also remember that he always kept a stash of tuna, soda, and other food supplies under his bed, just in case he needed to hole up in his room for a few days, I suppose. There were things under Artie's dresser, as there are under Harvey's, that no one could define. As you can tell, I didn't have to go very far to imagine the mess in Harvey's room.

Well, when Harvey's done cleaning, he calls his mother in to inspect his work. But how can she not notice the lumps under his rug? And this is why I decided to conclude the book with a question, "The End?" For Harvey it clearly isn't.

When I'm working on a book, I like to think about the kids who are going to read it. If a book I'm doing entertains me, makes me respond and feel in some way, even makes me chuckle out loud, then I can be pretty sure that it's going to entertain kids too. That's the one rule of thumb I've learned to follow as I continue making books.

BOOKS BY PAT CUMMINGS

Writer and illustrator

Jimmy Lee Did It. New York: Lothrop, 1985.

C.L.O.U.D.S. New York: Lothrop, 1986.

Clean Your Room, Harvey Moon! New York: Bradbury, 1991.

Petey Moroni's Camp Runamok Diary. New York: Bradbury, 1992.

Carousel. New York: Bradbury, 1994.

Illustrator

Good News. Written by Eloise Greenfield. New York: Coward, 1977.

Beyond Dreamtime: The Life and Lore of the Aboriginal Australian. Written by Trudie MacDougall. New York: Coward, 1978.

The Secret of the Royal Mounds. Cynthia Jameson. New York: Coward, 1980.

Just Us Women. Written by Jeannette Caines. New York: Harper, 1982.

My Mama Needs Me. Written by Mildred Pitts Walter. New York: Lothrop, 1983.

Fred's First Day. Written by Cathy Warren. New York: Lothrop, 1984.

Chilly Stomach. Written by Jeannette Caines. New York: Harper, 1986.

Springtime Bears. Written by Cathy Warren. New York: Lothrop, 1986.

I Need a Lunch Box. Written by Jeannette Caines. New York: Harper, 1988.

Storm in the Night. Written by Mary Stolz. New York: Harper, 1988.

Willie's Not the Hugging Kind. Written by Joyce Durham Barrett. New York: Harper, 1989.

Two and Too Much. Written by Mildred Pitts Walter. New York: Bradbury, 1990.

Go Fish. Written by Mary Stolz. New York: HarperCollins, 1991.

C is for City. Written by Nikki Grimes. New York: Lothrop, 1995.

Compiler and editor

Talking with Artists. New York: Bradbury, 1991.

Talking with Artists: Volume Two. New York: Simon & Schuster, 1995.

ABOUT PAT CUMMINGS

Pat Cummings has received many honors for her work. She won the Coretta Scott King Award for Illustration for her pictures in Mildred

Pitts Walter's *My Mama Needs Me*. The Coretta Scott King Award Committee also has honored her for *Just Us Women* by Jeannette Caines, *Storm in the Night* by Mary Stolz, and *C.L.O.U.D.S.*

Talking with Artists, a collection of conversations with children's book illustrators, which she compiled, received the 1992 *Boston Globe-Horn Book* Award for Nonfiction, and was named a *School Library Journal* Best Book of the Year, an American Library Association Notable Book, and a *Booklist* Editor's Choice. The second volume of *Talking with Artists* has met with similar critical acclaim.

A graduate of Pratt Institute, Pat Cummings has had her work exhibited in galleries throughout the country.

"Global Visuals" is adapted from a slide presentation she gave as a featured speaker at the seventh Virginia Hamilton Conference on April 5, 1991.

Brown Honey in Broomwheat Tea by Joyce Carol Thomas, illustrated by Floyd Cooper.

4

EXPLORING CULTURES
AN ARTIST'S STORY
FLOYD COOPER

WHEN I BEGIN an illustration, I select a piece of illustration board and I brush the complete surface with oil blotch. Using a kneaded eraser (which is a piece of rubber that does not contain sand), I begin to erase the paint from the board. For instance, if I want to make a face, I begin erasing at the top for the head and the paint is easily removed. I move down and create the features for the face very quickly. I put the nose on really fast and then the cheeks, and the face begins to appear. As I erase the paint from the board, the white of the illustration board shows through. If you erase really hard, you can almost get back to the original white surface of the board. All the dark areas on the board you leave alone, so there is less work to do for the background. Minute details can be achieved by just using the eraser, and many textures can be achieved. After the detail work is completed, you begin a process of building up oil glazes to add colors. The background oil wash is still evident as the color is applied, and the illustration can then be topped with a sponge, acrylic, chalk, or another medium. When the oil glaze (such as dry brush oils) is dry to the touch you can begin to erase more images out in the paint. This technique can also be done with pastels if you're working with small children. Just rub the pastel all over the piece of paper and use the eraser to erase an image out of it. It is an interesting technique for people at any level because it can go in so many different directions. It is very commonly used in the advertising industry. You may not recognize this technique because it can take on many different forms.

Even a water-based medium can be used. After the wash is dry, use acrylic watercolor washes. It is a versatile sort of medium. Someone asked what happens if I make a mistake. You can actually patch a part of it and correct mistakes just by brushing over the area and erasing again. I learned this technique at Hallmark, where I was an apprentice to Mark English, a famous illustrator. He came in to do a workshop which I was not allowed to go to because I had a more menial job redoing other people's artwork. English saw some of my work, however, and he asked me to help him do some jobs, a very lucky break for me. I learned this technique from the master and now I'm passing it on to everyone else.

I actually began drawing when I was three years old, and I can still remember scribbling a big bird on the side of my father's house. He didn't like that very much. I wasn't discouraged, though, and kept drawing all through school and eventually began a career at Hallmark Cards. I began to work professionally as an artist with Hallmark in Kansas City, creating ideas for greeting cards with pencil sketches. These would be sent to a committee, and they would decide whether or not the idea would become a card. Some ideas were rejected, so you would begin others. After awhile, I left Hallmark and began freelance artwork in the Kansas City area, with the opportunity to work on a number of major accounts. One was for a butter company, where I revised the logo, and another was some work for a movie called *Shogun*. My first use of the oil brush technique was done for an insurance company brochure.

While freelancing, I began to build my portfolio with a number of samples of my work. When I moved to New York City, I began to take this work around the city with the hopes of finding more freelance work. Illustrators usually take their portfolio around from place to place, but I wasn't having much success and the money was running out, so I employed an agent. Having an agent allowed me to stay home and do my artwork while the agent went out and acquired work for me. I began to pick up speed at that point. I was able to work very quickly and learned that the faster you work, the more money you make. At this time, I had a number of pieces that appeared in textbooks and work manuals, and all were done using the eraser technique. One piece won me acceptance into the Society of Illustrators. At about this time I began to do book jackets for children's books, such as Judy Blume's *Waiting for the Rain*.

After working on a number of book jackets, my agent sent me a manuscript and asked if I would be interested in trying the illustrations. Now you may recall that I mentioned I worked very fast in those days, and I didn't realize that what I was working on was a picture book. I finished the artwork in just four days (I was also a lot younger then) and returned it to my agent. The book was returned to me later with my name on it. It was *Chita's Christmas Tree*, about a little girl and her father as they look for the perfect Christmas tree.

The next books I illustrated were *Grandpa's Face,* about a little girl who is unsure of the faces her Grandpa makes, and *Laura Charlotte,* which describes a mother's love for a toy elephant she was given as a child, a gift she now passes on to her daughter. These two were followed by *Martin Luther King Jr. and His Birthday.* Then came *Pass It On* which is a collection of African American children's poetry. My first award-winning book was *Brown Honey in Broomwheat Tea,* which won the Coretta Scott King Honor for illustration. It is a collection of poems by Joyce Carol Thomas exploring the theme of African American identity. The little girl used in the illustrations for this book has posed for my work a number of times, and you may recognize her in other books.

I would like to share some tips on exploring a culture, which is what I've been doing with my art. I like to delve into cultures and explore them through my art, but you must be careful. When I was creating the artwork for *The Girl Who Loved Caterpillars,* for example, I had already been to Japan a few times, had spent many hours researching Japanese society, and had visited many libraries for information. I thought I was really ready to take on this job. I did all the paintings, and then I had the opportunity to meet Junko Yokota. My life became two parts then, before I met Junko and then after I met her. She pointed out some errors in the illustrations, and she taught me to pay the closest attention to detail when exploring a culture. For instance, in *The Girl Who Loved Caterpillars,* the kimono was originally crossed the wrong way. I had crossed it right over left and it should be left over right. Right over left in Japan means you're dead. I had to go back to the illustrations and make that important correction and others, including some work on the buildings. *The Girl Who Loved Caterpillars* is an adaptation of an anonymous twelfth-century Japanese tale about a young woman who resists social and family pressures as she befriends caterpillars and other socially unacceptable creatures.

Another title I illustrated was *Be Good to Eddie Lee,* a true story about a little boy with Down's syndrome. I visited with the boy and learned a lot about him, and I actually shot photographs of him at his school. In this story, Eddie Lee's sister, Christy, considers him a pest, until Eddie Lee shares several special discoveries with her. Then there was *Meet Danitra Brown,* written by Nikki Grimes, which introduces us to the world of a young African American girl through poetry.

I've also begun to write. My first book is *Coming Home: From the Life of Langston Hughes,* which is based on the life of Hughes as a young boy. It is also done in the oil wash and eraser technique. Writing and illustrating is such satisfying work that I look forward to making this an integral part of my career.

BOOKS BY FLOYD COOPER

Illustrator

Grandpa's Face. Written by Eloise Greenfield. New York: Philomel, 1988.

Chita's Christmas Tree. Written by Elizabeth Fitzgerald Howard. New York: Bradbury, 1989.

Laura Charlotte. Written by Kathryn O. Galbraith. New York: Philomel, 1990.

Martin Luther King, Jr. and His Birthday. Written by Jacqueline Woodson. New York: Silver, 1990.

When Africa Was Home. Illustrated by Karen Lynn Williams. New York: Orchard, 1991.

Imani's Gift at Kwanzaa. Written by Denise Burden-Patmon. Morristown, NJ: Modern Curriculum, 1992.

Dara's Cambodian New Year. Written by Sothea Chiemruom. Morristown, NJ: Modern Curriculum, 1992.

The Girl Who Loved Caterpillars: A Twelfth-Century Tale from Japan. Adapted by Jean Merrill. New York: Philomel, 1992.

From Miss Ida's Porch. Written by Sandra Belton. New York: Four Winds, 1993.

Be Good to Eddie Lee. Written by Virginia Fleming. New York: Philomel, 1993.

Pass It On: African-American Poetry for Children. Selected by Wade Hudson. New York: Scholastic, 1993.

Brown Honey in Broomwheat Tea: Poems. Written by Joyce Carol Thomas. New York: HarperCollins, 1993.

Meet Danitra Brown. Written by Nikki Grimes. New York: Lothrop, 1994.

Happy Birthday, Dr. King! Written by Kathryn Jones. New York: Simon & Schuster, 1994.

Daddy, Daddy, Be There. Written by Candy Dawson Boyd. New York: Philomel, 1995.

Jaguarundi. Written by Virginia Hamilton. New York: Blue Sky Press, 1995.

Coyote Walks on Two Legs. Compiled by Gerald Hausman. New York: Philomel, 1995.

Papa Tells Chita a Story. Written by Elizabeth Fitzgerald Howard. New York: Simon & Schuster, 1995.

How Sweet the Sound: African American Songs for Children. Selected by Wade and Cheryl Hudson. New York: Scholastic, 1995.

Pulling the Lion's Tale. Written by Jane Kurtz. New York: Simon & Schuster, 1995.

Gingerbread Days: Poems. Written by Joyce Carol Thomas. New York: HarperCollins, 1995.

The Story of Jackie Robinson. Written by Margaret Davidson. Milwaukee, WI: Gareth Stevens, 1996.

One April Morning: Children Remember the Oklahoma City Bombing. Written by Nancy Lamb and the Children of Oklahoma City. New York: Lothrop, 1996.

Writer and Illustrator

Coming Home: From the Life of Langston Hughes. New York: Philomel, 1994.

ABOUT FLOYD COOPER

Floyd Cooper began drawing at the age of three. He attended the University of Oklahoma on an art scholarship and later worked for Hallmark Cards. In 1985, Floyd moved to New York City, where he became acquainted with the world of children's books. His 1993 collaboration with Joyce Carol Thomas, *Brown Honey in Broomwheat Tea: Poems*, won Coretta Scott King honors for both writing and illustration.

This chapter is adapted from an art demonstration and slide presentation Floyd Cooper made as a featured speaker at the tenth Virginia Hamilton Conference on April 15, 1994.

Faithful Friend by Robert D. San Souci, illustrated by Brian Pinkney.

5

THE RHYTHM OF MY ART

BRIAN PINKNEY

I WOULD LIKE to share the technique I have been using to illustrate children's books. I use a scratchboard that comes from England and a razor-sharp scratchboard tool available in art supply stores. I begin with a dark surface and I scratch into that surface, using the tool. While I'm scratching out the images, I'm also thinking about light sources. It is almost as if you were in a very dark room and you began turning the lights up very slowly. First, you would see the light start to fall on objects like someone's forehead, so that is how I begin scratching. I also like using little lines, which is nice because I use a lot of lines to do a book. It can get boring scratching out the design, but when there are a lot of small lines to work on, it is almost a rhythmic instrument. When the image has been completely scratched out, you have a visible white image on the dark surface left. I add the colors next; this is the last part. I use oil paint and oil pastels and I rub the color over the image. Then I wipe the excess away with a damp cloth. With the latest books I have been working on, I have been going back over the image again with oil paint and the colors have been much brighter.

One of my favorite artists, of course, is my father Jerry Pinkney. He has had a lot of influence on me and on my decision to become an artist. One of the ways he influenced me when I was growing up was by letting me do what I wanted to do in my art. We would go to a museum or an art gallery and look at pictures, and then we would come home and everyone in our family would make pictures. When people ask me if I knew I wanted to become an artist or did my father influence me, I say I really always was an artist. I never saw being an artist as something that had to wait until adulthood because art was something we always did in the family. I also had a lot of validation in school.

Another very important artist, scientist, and musician I admired was Leonardo da Vinci. What I liked about Leonardo was that he was a scientist, and at a very young age I wanted to be a scientist. I was also going to be a musician and then, of course, an artist. I once did a report on Leonardo for school. When I was in school, I used to make drawings in my notebooks all the time, up and down the sides of the pages in the margins. Teachers didn't care for that too much, but what they did suggest was that I create illustrations for my reports. For my report on Leonardo, I copied a portrait that he had done, included some drawings of his little scientific instruments, and wrote about the musical instruments he played. Leonardo would also write backwards because he was lefthanded, and I began to write all my class notes backwards. Writing backwards worked really well until it was time to study for a test. I had to hold my notes up to a mirror to study them.

I'm always thinking about work. When I go to the beach, I can't enjoy myself, because I'm thinking about work. I usually bring along a sketchbook—even to the beach. I have over 40 sketchbooks now, dating back to when I was an undergraduate. I just do sketches. Even while I was riding in from the airport yesterday, I was looking at trees because I'm working on a book, and I have to illustrate a particular tree. I was looking at trees and houses, and as soon as I got back to the hotel, I sketched many of the things I had seen.

I began illustrating as soon as I graduated from college in 1983. I moved back in with my parents. My father has a studio downstairs and I had a studio upstairs. He was very proud that his son was following in his footsteps. Usually, I go into my studio at about five o'clock in the afternoon and I'll work straight into the night, often until two in the morning. My father is a very diligent worker; he is in his studio by 8:30 in the morning. He would go down to his studio and work for a few hours, and then he would come upstairs and check on me. Of course, I would still be in bed, and I would hear him coming up the steps. I would jump out of the bed and pull out all the work I had done the night before and start working on it so he could be proud of me. After about a year of living with my parents, I moved to Manhattan.

The first book I illustrated was *The Boy and the Ghost* by Robert D. San Souci. The process used in that book was very similar to scratchboard. I remember the night I came up with the concept of how I wanted to do the book. It is really important to me for the books to be personal in some way. In this case, it was eleven o'clock at night and I couldn't think of an idea for this story. When I went to bed very late that night, I closed my eyes and the first image came into my head. I jumped out of bed, ran to the studio, and drew it. Nothing else came, so I went back to bed, closed my eyes, and then the second image came. I jumped up and sketched the second image. By this time, I was getting the hint, so I turned the light off, jumped back into bed, and the third image came. For about an hour, I laid out the whole structure of the book this way, jumping in and out of bed. This book basically works the way a theatre does, like a stage, with the characters entering from stage left and moving around the stage and exiting stage right.

When I was little, I used to model for my father all the time. So if you think about his books where there is a little child in Africa or in India, then it is probably me. Sometimes when my sister was not around, I even had to model as a little girl. So, when I did my first book, who do you think I had model for the ghost in *The Boy and the Ghost*? For this book I was working in pencil and watercolor, which is very similar to the way my father works. But at the same time I had a knack for always putting in a lot of lines. I would build up form with line, not so much like cross-hatching, but like engraving. I had art directors who would tell me that I was using too many lines; you've got to get rid of those lines. I wasn't sure which lines to get rid of.

I received my master's degree from the School of Visual Arts, and while I was there an instructor introduced me to scratchboard. When using this technique, the more lines I put down, the lighter the image became. This technique felt so natural to me, it was almost like carving, engraving, or etching. I just fell in love with scratchboard. While I was in school, I illustrated *The Ballad of Belle Dorcas,* which was an important book to me because I had to do a lot of research about the South. As I am from Boston and New York, I did not know much about the South. I went to a family reunion in North Carolina and did all the sketches and took photos down there. Then I came back and illustrated the book. I found out two years later that this story actually originated twenty miles from where my mother was born, which is exactly where this family reunion took place, so the vegetation is all accurate. For models for this book, I used Andrea, my fiance at the time, and myself, because it was a love story.

At the School of Visual Arts there was a program of visual essays that I participated in. We had to create a series of images that were related in some way. These images had to tell a story without words. This project became a self-portrait for me. It was basically a series of images called "After the Marching Stopped," which was based on growing up after the Civil Rights Movement. I grew up in upstate New York and I went to integrated schools there. The experience of being different and then of finding out about my own history when researching *Belle Dorcas* made this book a very important project.

Around the time I created the images for "After the Marching Stopped," I was offered *Where Does the Trail Lead?* The story line did not mention a character, but when I read it, I saw myself as a child playing in Cape Cod. I decided I would do all the images with this little child playing around the sand dunes. When I was a child we would jump off the dunes and try to reach the water, and back then the dunes were really high, maybe thirty feet. I went to Cape Cod to do research for this book, and I found out the dunes are now only about waist high because of erosion. I created a number of sketches before I began the scratchboard for *Where Does the Trail Lead?* I often do fifteen to thirty sketches for each illustration, and each time I create another illustration of the same image, the picture becomes clearer. I then find a model and the illustration becomes even clearer. I'm then ready to transfer the image to scratchboard.

Sukey and the Mermaid by Robert D. San Souci was another book I created during this time. It is about a little girl who befriends a mermaid. The models in this book were very important because I needed a beautiful woman to be the mermaid, so, of course, I used my wife Andrea for the model. For the little girl in the story, I used my niece Gloria.

My first animal book was *The Elephant's Wrestling Match* by Judy Sierra. When I read the story I was excited about the idea of creating the animals. I went to *National Geographic* and bought their videos and watched them all day long. I spent a lot of time researching the animals in the story.

When I was young, I had a number of stuffed monkeys. I didn't have bears or other animals, only monkeys. So I based the drawing of the monkey on these stuffed animals. As usual, I took my sketches up to show my father and get his opinion. He looked at all the drawings and said, "You know, the elephant looks great. The crocodile is fantastic. But, there's something wrong with that monkey. It looks like those stuffed animals you used to have in your room." Of course, I had to go back to the library and research what a real monkey looks like. The talking drum in the story I actually got when I was on a press trip for *Essence Magazine*.

The first book I created with my wife was *Alvin Ailey.* Andrea wrote the book. She had been writing magazine articles for several years, and we decided we wanted to do a project together. I, of course, had all these great ideas for books but she didn't want to write them. And, of course, she had ideas that I didn't necessarily want to illustrate. At the time, we were taking dance lessons at one of the studios in Manhattan. We both love to dance. It happened that the instructor was one of the original dancers in the Alvin Ailey troupe. We decided to do a book on Alvin Ailey. When I was creating the illustrations, I really wanted the feel of Alvin Ailey, so I found all the videos that showed him dancing. I would go to performances and I'd practice the dances around the living room before Andrea came home from work. As I got the feeling for the illustrations, I decided to use myself as the model for Alvin Ailey, and Andrea modeled for the female dancers.

Our second book together was *Seven Candles for Kwanzaa*. At this point we decided that Andrea would write the book and when it was written, I would decide if I would illustrate it. After she finished writing, I couldn't imagine someone else illustrating this book. I fell in love with the story and decided to do the artwork. A lot of people ask what it's like working together as a couple. It's interesting. We actually work very well now, but we did have to come up with some guidelines, including formal meetings at the dining room table for our books. *Seven Candles for Kwanzaa* is a story that revolves around a family as they celebrate the holiday. I used African motifs in the borders. I actually found these motifs in Ghana. A four-year-old boy was the model for the main character in the book.

Another book that Andrea and I did together was *Dear Benjamin Banneker*, about the astronomer who corresponded with Thomas Jefferson. To research this book, we visited Annapolis and other sites in Maryland. We looked for the exact place where Benjamin Banneker's house used to be, but all we could find was a suburban neighborhood with people's backyards that we couldn't get into. But it was helpful being in that area and trying to picture what it was like to be Benjamin Banneker.

The last book I'll discuss is called *Max Found Two Sticks*, a book that I wrote. It's about a little boy who is a lot like me. I thought originally I wanted to do a wordless picture book so I wouldn't have to write anything, but since the book is about sounds, I realized it had to have sounds to describe the sounds that Max was making with his sticks. I thought about a drum teacher I once had, who said if you could sing a beat, then you could play it. From there on, I thought, okay, this is a way to write the sounds for this book. The artwork in this book has much brighter colors than some of my others, because I went back over the wash on the scratchboard with oil paint. *Max Found Two Sticks* is also set in the Brooklyn neighborhood where I now live. This book includes the street that I live on and the F train that I take when I am going into the city.

As I look to the future, I see myself writing more books in which the pictures and words work together. I also plan on doing more projects with my wife, Andrea.

BOOKS BY BRIAN PINKNEY

Writer and illustrator

Max Found Two Sticks. New York: Simon & Schuster, 1994.

Jojo's Flying Side Kick. New York: Simon & Schuster, 1995.

Illustrator

Julie Brown: Racing with the World. Written by R.R. Knudson. New York: Viking Kestrel, 1988.

The Boy and the Ghost. Written by Robert D. San Souci. New York: Simon & Schuster, 1989.

Harriet Tubman and Black History Month. Written by Polly Carter. New York: Silver, 1990.

The Ballad of the Belle Dorcas. Written by William H. Hooks. New York: Knopf, 1990.

Where Does the Trail Lead? Written by Burton Albert. New York: Simon & Schuster, 1991.

A Wave in Her Pocket: Stories from Trinidad. Written by Lynn Joseph. New York: Clarion, 1991.

The Lost Zoo. Written by Christopher Cat and Countee Cullen. Morristown, NJ: Silver Burdett, 1992.

The Dark Thirty: Southern Tales of the Supernatural. Written by Patricia C. McKissack. New York: Knopf, 1992.

Sukey and the Mermaid. Written by Robert D. San Souci. New York: Four Winds, 1992.

The Elephant's Wrestling Match. Written by Judy Sierra. New York: Lodestar, 1992.

Alvin Ailey. Written by Andrea Davis Pinkney. New York: Hyperion, 1993.

Seven Candles for Kwanzaa. Written by Andrea Davis Pinkney. New York: Dial, 1993.

Happy Birthday, Martin Luther King. Written by Jean Marzollo. New York: Scholastic, 1993.

Cut from the Same Cloth: American Women of Myth, Legend, and Tall Tale. Collected and retold by Robert D. San Souci. New York: Philomel, 1993.

The Dream Keeper and Other Poems. Written by Langston Hughes. New York: Knopf, 1994.

Dear Benjamin Banneker. Written by Andrea Davis Pinkney. New York: Harcourt, 1994.

Day of Delight: A Jewish Sabbath in Ethiopia. Written by Maxine Rose Schur. New York: Dial, 1994.

The Faithful Friend. Written by Robert D. San Souci. New York: Simon & Schuster, 1995.

Bill Pickett, Rodeo Ridin' Cowboy. Written by Andrea Davis Pinkney. New York: Harcourt, 1996.

When I Left My Village. Written by Maxine Rose Schur. New York: Dial, 1996.

Wiley and the Hairy Man. Retold by Judy Sierra. New York: Lodestar, 1996.

ABOUT BRIAN PINKNEY

Brian Pinkney has been interested in art since childhood. Influenced by his father, Jerry Pinkney, he continued his love for art throughout his youth and young adulthood. He received a master's degree from the School of Visual Arts in New York City and has twice won Coretta Scott King Honor awards for illustration for *Sukey and the Mermaid* and *The Faithful Friend. The Faithful Friend* was also named a Caldecott Honor book for 1996. His books regularly appear on a variety of notable book lists.

This chapter is adapted from the art demonstration and slide presentation Brian Pinkney made as a featured speaker at the tenth Virginia Hamilton Conference on April 15, 1994.

Scooter by Vera B. Williams.

6

PICTURING IMAGES OF A CHILDHOOD

VERA B. WILLIAMS

A BOOK, to me, is a little world. You can have it close, it's an intimate experience, and every element in it—the size, the weight, the paper, the type—constitutes this special little place that we get to create. The wonderful thing about a book is that it gets remade each and every time someone moves through it. I make the book, but my readers and viewers also make it through what they contribute to it. And the book is never quite the same again.

I want to talk about the way the culture of my childhood has presented itself in the little worlds of my books. I have very vivid memories of my little self, my childish self, not in a particularly ethnic way, but as a very eager and hopeful child growing up in a working-class family. These were the years of the Great Depression, and along with so many other people in this country, my family had to face the terrible struggle and suffering of trying to make a living, trying to find a job, trying to get enough money just to get by. That concern with making a living was very much woven into my childhood, and I think that there is a quality that runs through the life of people, no matter what color they are or where they live, when they have to struggle to survive.

I am thinking here of certain experiences that were so familiar to me as a child in a poor, working-class family, but I couldn't find these experiences in children's books when I started doing books of my own. I recall simple things, like sleeping on the sofa in the living room. So many people in children's books have a room of their own. We never had rooms of our own. People in children's books often have big houses with lots of space. We always lived in very crowded places. We moved a lot too. We moved a lot partly because my parents were rolling stones. But we also moved from place to place because we couldn't pay the rent or because there might be a better job somewhere else. Experiences like these gave a context to my life as a child, and I wanted them to be in my books. This sounds intentional, and I'm usually not a very intentional person. My intentions are strong, but they're not always very clear to me. Yet, when I started to make children's books, the qualities and experiences of my early life wanted to be told.

In the series of books I did—*A Chair for My Mother, Something Special for Me,* and *Music, Music for Everyone*—we have the story of the family of a waitress. To talk about people who are everywhere around us, but who are often not found in books for children was a desire of mine as a writer and illustrator. Well, I was very aware that women have been waitresses for a long time, if not for pay outside the home, then certainly in the home. And I wanted to acknowledge this ordinary role not as a grim critical statement about women, but as a reminder about life, about occupation, about surviving from day to day. Mother is a waitress in this series. It isn't discussed, and it isn't a problem. It's simply what she does. And she's lucky because she has a nice boss.

In *A Chair for My Mother,* the entire story has to do with filling a jar with money. While there are people in this book, two of the major characters are a jar and a chair. I sometimes think of the jar, the chair, and the mother as one person, although I didn't have this in mind before I made the book. But now that it's finished, it does seem to me that the jar, when it is still empty, and the chair, before the family buys it, are a whole. And the qualities of struggle and loss in the book and of not having what you want or need come from the fire, the empty jar, and needing that chair. In the fire, the furniture was burned up, and now the mother and grandmother have nowhere to sit except on a hard chair. Coming up with the money to get a new chair is a big deal for this family.

People often ask me, "Did you have such a chair when you were growing up?" No, I didn't have a chair like this one. Actually, we didn't have many chairs because we moved all the time. But that's the wonderful thing about a story. You can make up details when you're writing and you can imagine them when you're painting. You can write or paint something that is very autobiographical, even though it didn't really happen. These details, these experiences, come from a need. Wanting it to be a full jar. Wanting there to be such a chair. Wanting my mother not to have to work so hard and to have a wonderful place to sit down. It's interesting to think about these things, because you can see the ways in which experiences from your childhood, or perhaps even from the period in which you're actually making a book, feed into your stories and pictures in layers. Layers, though, may be too clear a stratification, because these details and images just tumble in, and once they do, they're immediately transformed into something bigger, something universal. So, while many images in my books are not necessarily autobiographical, each book is autobiographical in that it is rooted in my experiences as a child in a family that was very concerned with how we were going to survive on a day-to-day-basis.

The situations in my books end happily because the problems develop in joyous, satisfying ways. This type of resolution is in my books because, in a way, my stories are utopian. One of the qualities I think it is so important for children, and for all of us, to see is a genuine optimism, the kind of optimism which says that it is possible to change the world. Without optimism and hope, children can't be children and the heart dies. I was taught that ideology from an early age; it's very much in me and in my books. For me, an important theme that runs through this ideology has much to do with the neighborhoods in which I grew up. I saw plenty of hardworking people in those places. Even the people who were out of work but were looking for jobs were earnest when they could have been overcome by discouragement. How people live in these neighborhoods is a big interest of mine. We refer to such places as the inner city. We say that many of the children there are at-risk. Too often, we talk of such places as though we're talking about a problem for social workers. Of course, social workers in cities must deal with problems in droves, but that is only one part of the story.

I'm talking here about the way people become stereotyped and stigmatized as members of society who will not help themselves. But how could city neighborhoods survive if people were not constantly helping one another? There is an immense web of support in neighborhoods where people live on little money. "Do you have a few dollars until payday?" "Could your son come over and change my tire?" "Would you watch my kid? I have to take my other kid to the hospital." That kind of mutual aid makes up the lives of many people in urban neighborhoods and other environments. And it seems to me that this type of concern for others has gone on throughout history, and that it is as much a part of our national character as our tendency to be competitive and to make life hard for each other. This theme of support and caring is what I have always wanted to talk about and draw in my books.

I recently wrote a novel called *Scooter*. It's definitely an urban neighborhood book. In the story, I refer to the neighborhood setting as "the borough," but in my imagination it's a section of the Bronx, in New York City. The Bronx is where I spent a great deal of my childhood, and I was both deeply miserable and deeply happy there. *Scooter* takes place in a housing complex where life can be pretty difficult. Instead of talking about how dreadful it is to live in this place, I focus on the interactions among the people there. I reveal what they do, how they come to life, and how they realize their little lives. A lot goes on in their lives, but you never get the sense that you're in the midst of a desperate community. Perhaps it seems a little old-fashioned to some people to think in these ways in this day and age. I mean, where are the shootings and the drugs? Where are the horrible things that go on in a city? Well, I haven't written about them in this book. Instead, I focused on the quality that sustains us, which is our ability to do things together. And that's the quality I have put in many of my books. It's the sense of community, of concerned, caring people in an urban setting, that I wanted to make known in *Scooter* and in the other books I've done.

In several of my books there's a small detail, which, to me, reveals something significant about working-class people. This is the business of finding treasures in second-hand things. In *Three Days on a River in a Red Canoe*, you're looking at a secondhand canoe, and in *Something Special for Me*, it's a secondhand accordion that Rosa finally chooses as her prized birthday present. And then again in *Scooter*, Elana Rose, who wants some privacy in the small apartment she shares with her mother, finds one of those paneled screens in the garbage. Just what she needs to separate her small space from her mother's. A little detail like this can go a long way toward giving readers a sense of the culture in a book. A small touch like having characters search for used items out of necessity is what makes people and their culture come alive in a book, particularly when there are pictures to help do the telling. People buy used clothing. They have to. And it's a great coup when they find something good. The world of a book is made up of small details—graphic details, psychological details, social details. And all of these details together add up to a genuine world and an authentic community.

Sometimes you can use few details in the pictures and words and still suggest a great deal about people and their lives. *"More, More More," Said the Baby* demonstrates this. This, for me, is a different book, a departure of sorts. It grew out of an impulse different from the one that inspired my other books, although even here you can recognize some of the themes and impulses that connect my work. The impulse for this book was that I fell in love. I fell in love with my first grandchild, and I celebrate that here. We don't know a lot about the people in this book. Little Guy, Little Pumpkin, and Little Bird are the central characters, but I provide very few details about these children and the adults who are relating to them. I leave a lot unsaid. I wanted to put the imagination and feelings to work. Little Pumpkin, the black child, and Little Bird, the Asian child, I made from children I saw on the street in New York City, but Little Guy is more specific. He's my grandchild, and originally he was the only little person in the book.

Another "character" in *"More, More, More," Said the Baby* is color. I felt that color would talk to young children for whom words are new, and it would also convey my real love and excitement about the physicality and energy of Little Guy. There's no uncolored paper in this book. I did the color with gouache, which is thick watercolors, very much like the paints children use. I went out and got myself a new fat brush with a flicking point. Brushes are marvelous when they work. When their hairs fall out and they don't have points, they're awful. But when you have a good brush and this beautiful piece of paper, you have a joyous task ahead of you, which is very much how children go about painting. The joy of the paint, of the color, was, for me, one of the ways to celebrate Little Guy and, as it turned out, Little Pumpkin and Little Bird.

You'll notice that the dedication page reads, "For Hudson, For William, And for all our grandchildren." That last phrase is a bit ambiguous. By it I mean our grandchildren all over the world. Those small dots of different colors on the dedication page are meant to represent a worldwide community of grandchildren. Originally, I actually included the names for the colors—sienna, burnt sienna, umber, ivory, and so forth—but later I decided to replace all the words with dots, which I believe expresses the same idea.

When I began this project, I intended to have one child, Little Guy, spending some time with his father, his grandmother, and his mom, my daughter, who would come into the book at the very end. But in real life they all loved the baby so much that they called him all sorts of pet names. He was called "little pumpkin." He was "little bird." He was "little guy." After I had done the dummy of the book—the 32-page mock-up of it—and was well into telling the story, I realized that having one child in the book wasn't working for me. After all, the book wasn't going to be privately published for my family. People might get tired of looking at these same people. I needed a larger cast. With a larger cast I could show how the love I felt for this child was a universal feeling. Grandmothers of every shape, size, and hue, and grandfathers, fathers, and mothers, as well, all have similar feelings for their little guys, or, to use two Jewish words, their little *maziks* ("wild spirits"), their little *kaetzeles* ("pussycats"), or whatever else they call them all over the world. Isn't this business of generating names for their little ones one of the most creative, poetic things people do? From there, it really wasn't that difficult to change one story to three and the limited cast of characters to a fuller one. And this was partly due to the fact that what I had written was a small poem in three distinct sections, a poem, by the way, which came out very easily, because it came from the heart.

So, both a feeling and a concept led to the changes I made, and I believe these changes improved *"More, More, More," Said the Baby* in every way. For one thing, they made the book more interesting and more appealing to many different kinds of people. And they made the book more exciting to do. You'll notice, for example, that all the lettering is painted. That was a labor of love to commemorate this marvelous new birth. Not only did I paint the letters, but I painted all the way around them too, which was much more trouble. As I developed the book, I also played a lot with the backgrounds so that they seem to move, particularly because the background on a given page is often the only "furniture" in the picture, the only scenery. You'll also notice that the borders reverse. They're very similar, but within the similarity there's a lot of difference. They're similar enough to keep the book organized, and yet I got to play with the differences. That sense of difference within similarity goes through the entire book, through the graphics and through the people. I didn't use models or photographs to make the pictures, which is why I had to draw them over and over again. It took me a year to complete this book. I spent a lot of that time doing the lettering and working out the positions of the people. The writing for this book was easier to do than the illustrating.

We come full circle in *"More, More, More," Said the Baby.* The color, which I consider to be one of the characters, returns in the end to the big, swishy pinkness and the dots with which the book begins. But it doesn't stop with the final pages, because the story doesn't stop there. It carries on into the color of the flap and the back cover, which is very much a part of the world of the book. And there, finally, on the back of the book, we have the three pairs of characters again, a last reminder of the great love we've experienced in each of their stories. And this is my tribute to my first grandchild and "for all our grandchildren."

BOOKS BY VERA B. WILLIAMS

Writer and illustrator

It's a Gingerbread House: Bake It, Build It, Eat It! New York: Greenwillow, 1978.

The Great Watermelon Birthday. New York: Greenwillow, 1980.

Three Days on a River in a Red Canoe. New York: Greenwillow, 1981.

A Chair for My Mother. New York: Greenwillow, 1982. (In Spanish: *Un Sillon Para Mi Mama.* Live Oak Media).

Something Special for Me. New York: Greenwillow, 1983. (In Spanish: *Algo Especial Para Mi.* Morrow).

Music, Music for Everyone. New York: Greenwillow, 1984.

Cherries and Cherry Pits. New York: Greenwillow, 1986.

Stringbean's Trip to the Shining Sea. With Jennifer Williams. New York: Greenwillow, 1988.

"More, More, More," Said the Baby. New York: Greenwillow, 1990.

Scooter. New York: Greenwillow, 1993.

Lucky Song. New York: Greenwillow, 1997.

Illustrator

Hooray for Me! Written by Remy Charlip and Lilian Moore. Bowling Green, KY: Parents Press, 1975.

Our Class Presents Ostrich Feathers: A Play in Two Acts. Written by Barbara Brenner. Bowling Green, KY: Parents Press, 1978.

ABOUT VERA B. WILLIAMS

Since 1978, when she published *It's a Gingerbread House: Bake It, Build It, Eat It!,* the first book she both wrote and illustrated, Vera B. Williams has created many critically acclaimed picture books which celebrate community and family life among working-class people. Two of her books, *A Chair for My Mother* and *"More, More, More," Said the Baby,* were named Caldecott honor books. She has also twice received the *Boston Globe-Horn Book* Award; first for illustration for *A Chair for My Mother,* and recently, in the fiction category, for *Scooter.* She is also the recipient of the Parents' Choice Award for her illustrations for *Three Days on a River in a Red Canoe. Cherries and Cherry Pits* and *Stringbean's Trip to the Shining Sea,* a collaboration with her daughter, were both honored as best-illustrated books of the year by the *New York Times.*

A graduate in art from Black Mountain College, Vera B. Williams has lived on a houseboat in Vancouver Bay, British Columbia, co-founded and taught in alternative schools for children, and worked as a political activist promoting the causes of nonviolence, children, women, and the environment.

This chapter is adapted from the slide presentation she gave as a featured speaker at the tenth anniversary Virginia Hamilton Conference on April 15, 1994.

Navajo: Visions and Voices Across the Mesa by Shonto Begay.

7

REFLECTIONS FROM A HOLY SPACE

SHONTO BEGAY

YA' ATEEH, Nizhoui go' Ni Haa ni ya hiigi' ba' ah'enisin. That's Navajo for "Hello, everyone. I'm glad to be here, really proud, and I'm honored to be part of your conference." A more literal translation of this greeting is, "In an honorable and beautiful way, I am accepted here, and I humbly return the sentiment." The Navajo word *ya ateeh* has transcended the Navajo language to become a pan-American Indian greeting. *Ya' ateeh* translated literally means "holiness," harmony," "acceptance," and "hello." Among the Navajo people, everything wonderful is passed along through handshakes with everyone you meet. *Ya' ateeh* is a beautiful word, so now you can turn to your neighbor, shake hands, and say *Ya' ateeh*.

ΔΔΔ

As a product of the U. S. Government boarding school phenomenon in the 1960s, I was subjected to "B"-class western movies that featured a large cast of Native Americans. When I was a kid, I really believed that all Indian tribes across America spoke Navajo, because that was the language Native people usually spoke in the old westerns I saw in boarding school. In these movies, the Native Americans would be seen planning an invigorating war party that was supposed to take place the next day, and they would be talking to one another in their native language. All of my friends and I would laugh as we watched, because the actors weren't planning a battle. In our language, they were talking about what they were going to do with their money when they got paid. Being a part of the government boarding school situation, I was also subjected to very harsh treatment by the Bureau of Indian Affairs. At the time, we could be literally kidnapped off our land by government agents and sent to boarding school. Mothers and fathers who protested were often sent to jail. My parents spent many days in jail because they refused to send their children to one of those schools.

I come from a family of sixteen brothers and sisters and was raised in a traditional Navajo household. A hogan with no electricity and no running water is as traditional as you can get. My father is still practicing traditional Navajo medicine there. I grew up assisting my father in a lot of ceremonies, gathering herbal plants in summer and winter, offering prayers to these plants, and getting to know the relationships between plants, animals, and people. When I was a kid, this business of assisting my father was very tiring, monotonous hard work. I often thought, "Here we go again!" It wasn't until some years later that I came to realize how very fortunate I was to have been brought up this way.

I think I was also very fortunate to have been brought up without television, because this gave me the opportunity to train my vision. When I visit schools, I often tell kids that the best thing they can do for themselves is to turn off the television and find a holy spot, a holy ground, within their world. I have such a place in my own world, which I call my "Story Rock." You can see a painting of it on the title page in my book *Navajo*. I spent years on that rock tending sheep. It was a magic carpet on which I could fly all over the world and transcend time and space. On that rock I dreamed, I painted, I drew pictures, I read books, I schemed. A lot of the time, I'd get so involved in my thoughts that I'd look down to the valley below and the sheep would have moved into the cornfield. I often challenge kids to find a space like this. I sometimes receive a letter from one of these kids, that says, "I have found a space in my own life which I'm keeping holy. It's my dream place. It's my holy space." Of course, that makes all the road trips, all the different hotels I have to stay in, and all those connections at airports worth the energy.

In my book *Navajo*, which I both wrote and painted, my whole pursuit was to share the little world I come from. The Navajo world. The book is not meant to make readers experts on Navajo culture. It's just a small introduction, a little surface work on my culture. Through my illustrations and my words, I tried to show some of the pain and joy, the mythology and contemporary reality of Navajo life in one small book. I'm really proud of how *Navajo* turned out, and I credit a lot of its success to my editor, Dianne Hess. I tell her that *Navajo* is as much her book as it is mine, but, of course, she denies that.

"In My Mother's Kitchen" is one of the paintings in *Navajo* that is very personal for me. I did this painting because I attach some of my warmest feelings to experiences I had in this kitchen. I'll share with you the poem I wrote to accompany the painting.

In My Mother's Kitchen
Fragrance of fresh tortillas and corn stew
Fills my mother's kitchen
Sparsely furnished
Crowded with warmth
Soot-grayed walls, secretive and blank
She moves gently in and out of light
Like a dream just out of reach

The morning light gives her a halo
That plays upon her crown of dark hair
Strong brown hands caress soft mounds of dough
She gazes out into the warming day
Past sagebrush hills, out towards the foot of Black Mesa
How far would she let the goats wander today
Before it rains

Childhood dreams and warmth
Tight in my throat, tears in my eyes
The radio softly tuned to a local AM station
News of ceremonies and chapter meetings
And funerals
Flows into the peaceful kitchen
Lines upon her face, features carved of hard times
Lines around her eyes, creases of happy times
Bittersweet tears and ringing silvery laughter
I ache in my heart

My mother's gentle movements light up dark corners
Her gentle smiles recall childhood dreams still so alive
My mother moves in and out of light
Like clouds on days of promising rain

I did every one of the paintings for *Navajo* in my studio. Most of them I did with acrylic on canvas, but some are watercolors, and others are lithographs. I like to work in all mediums.

Ma'ii and Cousin Horned Toad, another book of mine, is also very personal. I heard the story from my grandmother many, many times. Inside this book is a song I wrote for Ma'ii, the trickster coyote. I made this song for him while he is scheming to find a way to trick Cousin Horned Toad out of some of his precious corn. This is a favorite book of a good friend of mine who teaches in Arkansas. When she first read the story with her students, she didn't know the tune of the song, so she put it to a country-and- western beat. She and her students sang it with a country twang for a long time until a tape of the song came out.

When she played it, her students turned to her and said, "I thought you said he wrote the book. He doesn't even know the song."

ΔΔΔ

Many of the American Indian dwellings called hogans are circular in order to imitate a model of the universe. Everything travels in a cycle. Everything comes back in a cycle. In our language there is no word meaning "goodbye." The closest we come to *goodbye* is *ha' goone'*, a term of acknowledgment meaning "Until we meet again. Until things come full circle." In Native cultures, the Circle of Life is a symbol for the Four Directions, which represent the four stages of life, from childhood to old age, and the cycle of the seasons, from spring to winter. The hogan doors always face East, for the East symbolizes knowledge. I was raised on the south side of a hogan, which is where all kids are raised, in the direction of life and innocence. The North to us is mystery and wisdom. A long time ago, when someone died in a hogan, the person was carried to the north wall and buried there. We believe that the spirit travels back to the North, back to the spirit world, but not back to the dark world. The West is the direction of holiness, strength, and the power of change, all conditions or qualities associated with the female.

In Navajo families, the mother is still considered the strongest. She owns the house and almost everything else. In the past, and much of this is still true today, when the mother got tired of anyone in the family, all she had to do was place that person's saddle outside the hogan door. That was final. Among the Navajo, as in most tribes, matrilineal tracing of families is still the custom. Whenever I meet somebody for the first time, I say I'm from Shonto, Arizona, which means "sparkles that play on the surface of the water when the sun hits it." I'm a member of the Bitter Water Clan, the *To' dii Chiini'* Clan. This is my mother's clan, my primary clan. My "born for" clan is my father's clan, the Salt Clan, which is *Ashii hi* in Navajo. My maternal grandfather was from the Many Goats Clan, the *Tlizi taani*. My paternal grandfather's clan is the *Tsi' najinni'*, the Black Streaked Wood people. People I've never met could very well be my clan sister, brother, aunt, or mother, and thus I must treat them as such. You really need to be careful, because you can never marry into your own clan or any of the four clans that make up your family on your mother's and father's sides. It so happens that the Bitter Water and the Salt Clans have the most people. It seems that every time I turn around, I meet people from these clans.

ΔΔΔ

Back in the 1970s, I was hired as a ranger for the U. S. Government National Parks Service up in the Grand Tetons, in Wyoming. For some reason, the government thought all Indians were alike. You know, if you're Indian, you're an expert in all aspects of life in all the tribes. I remember that I arrived in Grand Teton National Park on a very cloudy and cold June afternoon. It was still snowing. The first thing on my schedule was to do a teepee demonstration the next day. Now I had never set up a teepee in my life. Thanks to one of my co-workers, a Shoshone, I got a quick lesson in how to set up teepees, the stories behind them, and the appropriate directions and orientations for them. It was Saturday evening.

I woke up late the next morning, quickly got on my bike, and rushed down to the visitors' center. I should have been there half an hour earlier. The tarp and all the other materials for the demonstration were in a storeroom that happened to be behind the lectern in an amphitheater where an interdenominational church service was in full swing. The preacher standing at the lectern was addressing a congregation of about a thousand people. I was really looking the part of the pan-American Indian in my ribbon shirt and headband. To get into that storeroom, I had to move behind the preacher. I tried to pass behind him as quietly as I could. But there I was in full view of about a thousand people. I was so nervous, that as I tried to open the door, I dropped the key a few times. The preacher stopped the sermon and glared at me. When I finally got the door open, what I found in the storeroom wasn't a small canvas at all; it was this huge thing. As I dragged it out, it somehow unraveled behind me, catching the cord of the microphone and dragging it off the stage. As soon as I was out of sight, I took off like a wild man, but people were shouting behind me, "There's a microphone following you."

Of course, in all the confusion, I forgot everything I was taught the night before. When I went up to where I was supposed to do the teepee demonstration, I had no idea where to start. There I was, looking like everyone's version of an Indian and drawing a blank in front of all the people who had gathered. After telling the audience that a teepee is a very holy structure for people in the Plains, I informed the crowd that putting a teepee together is not a job for one person. Luckily, there were some mountain men in the audience. They lived in teepees year-round, so they were very proud of their expertise. They got that teepee up in a matter of minutes. "Yep, that's how we do it," I told the crowd.

I think this illustrates that you can't assume the American Indian culture is one thing. We are a very diverse people, and I represent only a small piece of it, and then again, only a small piece of the Navajo nation. Within today's Navajo nation there are at least 70 different clans, and there are several distinct dialects among speakers of the Navajo language.

ΔΔΔ

We're a real celebrating culture. Native peoples—and this is true of the Navajos as well—don't celebrate birthdays as an annual event. Instead, we celebrate the stages of life. For example, the birth itself and the first laugh are celebrated, and our coming of age ceremony is like a bar or bat mitzvah. We also mark the seasons, and since Christmas just happens to fall on one of those ceremonies, we began to include it in our celebration. The Navajo language and Navajo traditions are still very viable. My mother still weaves her rugs according to tradition, and my father still heals in traditional ways. In fact, he's probably needed more now than ever, because now we have to live in and acknowledge two worlds—the natural, ancient world of our people and the high-tech, contemporary world. A lot of Native people are victims of a collision of these two cultures. My father's journey, his entire mission, is to make this evolution and adjustment as positive as possible. What he does today through his counsel is to strive for balance and harmony between these two cultures. I think you also feel this struggle between the ancient and the contemporary in the words and pictures I did for *Navajo*.

ΔΔΔ

Growing up in a traditional Navajo household, you hear a lot of stories about *Ye' naal gloshi'*, Skinwalker, our version of the boogeyman. At night when kids refuse to sleep or are just plain restless, someone will warn them that if they don't behave, Skinwalker will get them. Skinwalker can cast spells. He can cause such disharmony within you that you can get sick. I grew up with this fear, although I never ran into Skinwalker personally. It seemed like everybody else was always running into him though. I couldn't decide whether everyone else was making up stories or whether I was just deprived. I spent years living in the Bay Area in San Francisco. I'd walk across the university green telling myself from time to time that there's no such thing as Skinwalker. Well, I managed to hold on to that belief for maybe five or ten minutes at a time. This belief, like many, many other pieces in my past, was so ingrained in me that I finally had to paint Skinwalker to make this childhood fear tangible. And it worked. I tell kids about the value of confronting childhood fears. If you name them, draw them even, you make them less threatening.

ΔΔΔ

I worked for ten years as a ranger in Grand Teton National Park in Wyoming and Grand Canyon National Park in Arizona. Just before I burned out and decided to leave this job, I was working at the Navajo National Monument on the Navajo Reservation in northern Arizona. The holy structures in the ancient ruins I saw in these sacred places are much like those of a church or synagogue. They are subterranean structures called kivas. The stories of the people who lived in these places are, of course, just as valid and vital as the stories of all ancient peoples. These are stories that teach while they entertain and often explain natural phenomena. The story I tell in *Ma'ii and Cousin Horned Toad* is no exception. When I tell this story in the schools I visit, I ask the kids what they learned from it. They say, "Don't be greedy," or "Don't try to cheat your cousin." For one little kid, the moral was, "Never swallow your cousin." I like that.

There are also stories about the Hero Twins, Monster Slayer and Born-for-Water, which I hope to tell and illustrate some day soon. These tales from Navajo mythology are about the reconquest of the third and fourth worlds and the deliverance of the people from evil monsters. They are the backbone of Navajo mythology and are just as complex and exciting as Greek myths. When we do ceremonies of healing, it is customary to replay the journey of the Hero Twins as a way of slaying our own demons, our fears, our disharmony. We do this to get everything back in order. Storytelling through ceremonies is to this day very important in my culture. I like to think that I carry on this tradition in my books. I like to think that through my art I am doing my part in making my culture known to others.

BOOKS BY SHONTO BEGAY

Writer and illustrator

Ma'ii and Cousin Horned Toad: A Traditional Navajo Story. New York: Scholastic, 1992.

Navajo: Visions and Voices Across the Mesa. New York: Scholastic, 1995.

Illustrator

The Mud Pony: A Traditional Skidi Pawnee Tale. Retold by Caron Lee Cohen. New York: Scholastic, 1988. (In Spanish: *El Poni de Barro*).

The Native American Book of Change. White Deer of Autumn. Hillsboro, OR: Beyond Words Publishing, 1992.

The Native American Book of Knowledge. White Deer of Autumn. Hillsboro, OR: Beyond Words Publishing, 1992.

The Native American Book of Life. White Deer of Autumn. Hillsboro, OR: Beyond Words Publishing, 1992.

The Native American Book of Wisdom. White Deer of Autumn. Hillsboro, OR: Beyond Words Publishing, 1992.

The Boy Who Dreamed of an Acorn. Written by Leigh Casler. New York: Philomel, 1994.

The Magic of Spider Woman. Written by Lois Duncan. New York: Scholastic, 1996.

ABOUT SHONTO BEGAY

Shonto Begay's artwork has been praised by critics throughout the southwestern United States for over twenty years, and many of his paintings have been selected for permanent museum collections. His love for art began in his youth, which he spent in northeastern Arizona's Klethla Valley, at the foothills of the Shonto Plateau. He later studied fine arts at the Institute of American Indian Arts in Santa Fe and at the California College of Arts and Crafts in Oakland, where he received his degree with distinction. *The Mud Pony,* his first illustrated book, was a *Reading Rainbow* selection, and *Ma'ii and Cousin Horned Toad,* the first book he both wrote and illustrated, won the 1993 Arizona Author Award. *Navajo: Visions and Voices Across the Mesa* was recognized by the American Library Association as a Notable Book for Children and a Best Book for Young Adults in 1996, and, in the same year, was chosen by the National Council for the Social Studies–Children's Book Council Joint Committee as a Notable Children's Book in the Field of Social Studies. "My illustrations for books," Shonto Begay has commented, "utilize a textured mixture of watercolor and colored pencils. My acrylic paintings, my larger pieces, are a series of brush strokes—small strokes repeating like the words of Blessingway prayers. For me the process is a visual chant. My works are personal visions shared."

"Reflections from a Holy Space" is adapted from the slide presentation Shonto Begay made as a featured speaker at the eleventh Virginia Hamilton Conference on April 21, 1995.

Vejigante Masquerader by Lulu Delacre.

8

A LATINA BUILDING BRIDGES

LULU DELACRE

I ONCE HEARD Rosa Angela Adoum, Director of Education and Culture in Quito, Ecuador, give a speech at a conference for bilingual educators. As an educator and anthropologist, she emphasized the fact that in her country, as in many Latin American countries, the keeper of the culture, its customs and traditions, is usually the mother. Her words rang true then and still resonate in my mind now.

I must admit that, prior to becoming a mother myself, I had not realized how important it is for me to keep alive the language and traditions I grew up with. My instinctive desire to share the folk songs and games of my childhood with my daughters, first generation born in the U.S., is what brought about the *Arroz Con Leche* collection. Knowing how little of this material the market had to offer made me reach for myself and other Latino mothers, reach for the joy an English-speaking mother feels when sitting side by side with her toddler singing Mother Goose rhymes while relishing that the picture book depicts children like her own.

I am very proud of *Arroz Con Leche*, this short collection of rhymes, because before it was published I could not find a book like it in the market— a book with both the songs and rhymes that I grew up with, as well as pictures of the children that sing them and of the places they come from. It gives me great pleasure to see how this book continues to sell and to have Latino mothers come to me and thank me because I have done something no one else had done before. I've done countless presentations on the making of a picture book, using *Arroz Con Leche* as a model. I still feel privileged to see the pride in the eyes of Latino children as I share in the dancing and the singing of the games. And I know I have helped non-Latino children to accept and appreciate Latino language and culture.

When I was researching the songs to include in *Arroz Con Leche*, I encountered many Christmas songs that I could not resist singing. These songs brought warm folk memories to me of Christmas in Puerto Rico, where I was born and raised. Christmas is a season rich in music in all of Latin America, with each country celebrating the same old folklore beliefs in their own colorful ways. As I collected these Christmas songs, I thought the holiday season deserved a book of its own, where I could illustrate and share the customs of different countries through accompanying songs. So *Las Navidades* was born. This book is more than a collection of Christmas songs. The songs are there as a way of sharing Latin American traditions, in some cases traditions that are slowly disappearing.

One of these traditions is Epiphany. In Puerto Rico we celebrate not only Three Kings Day, or Epiphany, but also the eight days after that, the *Octavas*, and then the *Octavitas*, eight days after that. So we keep on celebrating for sixteen days. We are a people who like to celebrate. In one part of the tradition, adults pray the rosary in front of the Magi's altar until dawn. Then we have a big banquet. Meanwhile, the children cut grass clippings and put them in shoeboxes, believing that the kings will come on horses, rather than on camels. The horses will eat the grass clippings in the shoeboxes, and in return, the kings will leave small toys in the shoeboxes for children. This is a tradition that I still keep alive at our home in Maryland, which of course is not without the problem of going out into six inches of snow for grass clippings, but I try to keep this tradition alive for my young daughters.

Another way to keep the culture alive is through the language. As Joseph Bruchac has mentioned, language carries much of the richness of a culture. That is one of the reasons I insisted that *Vejigante: Masquerader*, a book based on folklore, be a bilingual book. I often go to schools around the nation and give presentations showcasing *Vejigante: Masquerader*, a book in which the main character, Ramon, achieves his dream through persistence and help from a close community. When I read a few pages of the book, first in English and then in Spanish, it gives me great pleasure to watch the Latino children as their eyes perk up and their smiles broaden when listening to someone acknowledge the language spoken at home.

I truly believe that it is important to give these children that acknowledgment of their heritage. *Vejigante: Masquerader* is very special to me because it conveys my own belief that through persistence you really can achieve anything you want to achieve. This book takes place in Ponce, a city in the South of Puerto Rico. In Ponce the tradition of the vejigante masquerader is very special. The masqueraders come around not only during the carnival itself, which is held for seven days in the month of February, but for the whole month of February. It's a wonderful celebration. I hid 28 lizards in *Vejigante: Masquerader,* to represent the 28 days of February.

The Bossy Gallito is a Cuban retelling of a traditional cumulative tale. It tells of what happens to a rooster on his way to his uncle's wedding. Immediately after reading Lucia Gonzalez's retelling, I envisioned the book design to remind the reader of a wedding photo album. I even created borders for the pages. I set the story in a Cuban area of Miami, Florida, known as Calle Ocho, Little Havana. In order to conduct research, I attended a traditional Cuban wedding there. Then I met with Lucia Gonzalez to discuss the foods offered at weddings, and which was the best church facade to picture at the end of the book.

I tried to convey Cuban-American culture through the birds depicted in the book. For instance, in one scene four birds are playing dominos. Cuban-American men in Miami actually do enjoy playing dominos just as Cuban men in Havana do. The birds in *The Bossy Gallito* are all from the Miami area. The rooster does arrive in the story, in Latin American style: late for the wedding but in time for the party.

As a mother, I am constantly searching for books in Spanish for my own daughters, books that will acquaint them with their roots, with their parents' and grandparents' heritage. As a series of events led to my new book of Latin American folklore, I saw my oldest daughter read and reread a collection of tales from Europe, and I wished I could see a similar collection in Spanish of Latin American tales. Then I caught myself telling an old Puerto Rican legend to my youngest daughter on a trip to Puerto Rico. Finally, it was the advice of a knowledgeable friend who told me it is through their folktales that we know a people. All of these influences led me to create *Golden Tales: Myths, Legends and Folktales from Latin America*. It is by far the most complex book that I have ever done, fascinating, compelling, and a wonderful learning experience that I have just finished. The book is done in two versions, one in English and one in Spanish. The reader goes on a wonderful voyage, as the stories are set in the Caribbean and other areas in Latin America.

In the first section of *Golden Tales*, there are five stories from the lands of the Taino, the Indian peoples that originally inhabited the West Indies. In the introduction to this section, I tried to picture what we inherited from these ancient people, such as words, fruits and vegetables. We may have also inherited the good and hospitable nature that these kind people had. A myth in this section discusses how the sea was formed. For this book's illustrations I changed my art techniques. You will notice as you look at this book that it is not the same style of art that I have used before. The illustrations are oil paintings, which achieve the mystery and the magic that these tales have.

The second tale from the land of the Taino is the story of "Guanina," which is based on history and is a legend from Puerto Rico that dates back to 1511. Guanina fell in love with Don Cristobal de Sotomayor, a Spanish conquistador, and this story tells what happened to them. It is actually a love story. Don Cristobal dies in battle. Guanina knows she is not able to live without him, so she lies down beside him and also dies. They are buried together under a huge old ceiba tree, and legend says that on that spot fragrant white lilies and wild red poppies bloom year after year. Another Puerto Rican legend is "The Eleven Thousand Virgins," which is also based on historical events. An English general, Sir Ralph Abercromby sails with his 60 swift-sailing tall ships and fourteen thousand men and tries to conquer the beautiful Spanish colony of Puerto Rico. The legend says that the city was saved by a night of prayer, hope and eleven thousand lights. Two other Taino selections in the book include a Dominican legend from 1836, which is called "The Laughing Skull" and a Cuban folktale called "Sencion, the Indian Girl," about a girl of mixed-race heritage—black, white and Taino.

There are three tales in the book from the land of the Zapotec, including "When the Sun and the Moon Were Children" and "How the Rainbow Was Born." A third tale in this section is "The Miracle of Our Lady of Guadalupe," which I don't call a folktale or a myth, but rather a miracle. One tale in the book is from the land of the Muisca and is entitled "El Dorado." The book concludes with three tales form the lands of the Quechua, children of the Inca: "Manco Capac and the Rod of Gold," "Kakuy," and "The Courier."

In the back portion of *Golden Tales* there is a section titled "Notes and Sources," which highlights background information on each of the twelve tales in the four sections. Additionally, there is information on the symbolism in the artwork and information on art techniques used for each of the twelve stories in the book.

I believe there is a common thread weaving in and out of my books and that is the desire to show what I know of my culture through the richness of language, authentic details, and illustrations. Through my work, I try to convey to children the pride I feel in my heritage. I strongly feel that all children benefit from learning about their classmates' heritage. This knowledge can only begin to foster acceptance and respect among cultures. It is the duty of parents, educators, librarians, authors, and illustrators to bring children the books that will open their eyes to the wealth of what other people have to offer. To quote Virginia Hamilton: "After all, it is through the sharing of and learning about parallel cultures, that a child grows and discovers her world and enriches her life." Muchas gracias.

BOOKS BY LULU DELACRE

Written or retold and illustrated

ABC Rhymes. New York: Simon & Schuster, 1984.

Counting Rhymes. New York: Simon & Schuster, 1984.

Kitten Rhymes. New York: Simon & Schuster, 1984.

Lullabies. New York: Simon & Schuster, 1984.

Nathan & Nicholas Alexander. New York: Scholastic, 1986.

Nathan's Fishing Trip. New York: Scholastic, 1988.

Arroz con Leche: Popular Songs and Rhymes from Latin America. English lyrics by Elena Paz. Musical arrangements by Ana-Maria Rosado. New York: Scholastic, 1989.

Good Times with Baby. New York: Grosset & Dunlap, 1989.

Time for School, Nathan. New York: Scholastic, 1989.

Las Navidades: Popular Christmas Songs from Latin America. English lyrics by Elena Paz. Musical arrangements by Ana-Maria Rosado. New York: Scholastic, 1990.

Nathan's Balloon Adventure. New York: Scholastic, 1991.

Peter Cottontail's Easter Book. New York: Scholastic, 1991.

Vejigante: Masquerader. New York: Scholastic, 1993.

De Oro y Esmeraldas: Mitos, Leyendas y Cuentos Populares de Latinoamerica. New York: Scholastic, 1996.

Golden Tales: Myths, Legends and Folktales from Latin America. New York: Scholastic, 1996.

Sir Cat's Romance: and Other Favorite Stories from Latin America. New York: Scholastic, 1997.

Illustrated

Aloysius Sebastian Mozart Mouse. Written by Oretta Leigh. New York: Simon & Schuster, 1984.

The Tale of Peter Rabbit and Other Stories. Written by Beatrix Potter. Morristown, NJ: J. Messner, 1985.

The Wind in the Willows: The Open Road. Written by Kenneth Grahame. New York: Simon & Schuster, 1985.

Maria and Mr. Feathers. Written by Hannah Kimball. Morristown, NJ: Modern Curriculum, 1991.

The Bossy Gallito: El Gallo de Bodas; A Traditional Cuban Folktale. Retold by Lucia M. Gonzalez. New York: Scholastic, 1994.

ABOUT LULU DELACRE

Lulu Delacre's art has been exhibited in Puerto Rico, Washington D.C., New York, and Connecticut. She graduated with high honors from L'Ecole Superieure d' Arts Graphiques in Paris, where she earned a full scholarship for academic achievement. Born and raised in Puerto Rico, she has created many bilingual books that stem from her heritage. Her book *Vejigante: Masquerader* earned the 1993 American Book Award and was named a 1994 Notable Children's Book in the Language Arts by the Children's Literature Assembly of the National Council of Teachers of English. *The Bossy Gallito* was chosen as a 1996 Pura Belprè Honor Book for illustration by the Association for Library Service to Children (ALSC) and REFORMA, the National Association to Promote Library Services to the Spanish Speaking, an affiliate of the American Library Association. Lulu Delacre makes her home in Silver Spring, Maryland, with her husband and two daughters.

This chapter is adapted from a slide presentation which Lulu Delacre made as a featured speaker at the eleventh Virginia Hamilton Conference on April 21, 1995.

Pink and Say written and illustrated by Patricia Polacco.

9

HEROES

PATRICIA POLACCO

WHEN MY MOTHER'S people arrived in this country, all of the girls and women were wearing one of these head scarves. This head scarf has the same name as grandmother in Russia; it is called a babushka. The babushka is thrown over the head and pulled very tight against the forehead and then you twist, twist, twist the edges, you pull it forward and you tie it, but not down on the neck, up by the mouth. Then a woman would go out and work in the sun and pull a part out to shield her eyes. Even in the snow this is how it was worn. She would take it off from her chin and tuck it in when she came in the house, but she very rarely removed the babushka, because this symbolized for her the country that our family was forced to leave.

When my great-grandmother Anna came to this country, she was wearing a red babushka and a blue linen dress. She came with her mother, her father, and a sister. They landed on Ellis Island, and that is where we lost and gained our family name. We think our name might originally have been Guagashvillie but it was shortened to Gaw. Sometimes people thought they were being named by the government when they came. They had to leave behind grandmothers, grandfathers, aunties, uncles, cousins, and children. In those days when you left Russia, you never went back. It was the same as dying, so Anna's mother brought two burlap bags of the clothes of the people she loved, and she would take the clothes out and still smell the scent of the skin of that person and it helped her remember home. Almost every day Anna wore her little red babushka and the blue dress. She hated to take them away from her skin because she knew that if she gave them up she might give up home. The day came, of course, when she began to outgrow them, and she went to her mother and said, "Mama, what am I going to do? If I can't wear this dress, if I can't wear this babushka, I'm going to forget home." Her mother said, "Anna, I know a way." Her mother took out a pair of scissors and cut her babushka into pieces, and she took the scissors and cut the blue dress into pieces. Then she got the clothes from the two burlap bags and cut them into pieces. Then her mother called the other ladies and they got together and sewed all the pieces together into a quilt. The edge of the quilt was Anna's babushka, the inside was not only her dress but clothes from people back home. Anna's mother threw it over her shoulders and said, "Anna, when you miss home, touch the quilt. Run your fingers around the edges of the animals, but look at the material, remember the person who wore these clothes. If you can remember them, then you keep home in your heart." So in our family we called this the keeping quilt. I still have it to this day and I brought it to show to you. The edge of it is no longer Anna's babushka, because it had to be resewn 50 years ago. We do know, though, that anything that has blue linen is her dress.

When I was little, this was the quilt that I was raised with. I used to sleep always with the yellow horse by my face. Every night before I'd go to sleep, I'd run my fingers around the edge of this horse. Here's how wonderful memory is: When I touch this, I can still hear my grandmother coming up the wooden stairs. Sitting on the bed and saying, "Now Trisha whose dress made this?" And I'd look and I'd say, "Why that's Aunt Havela's." "And where is she?" "Well, she's back home in Russia." "Yes, and whose shirt is this?" "That is Uncle Vladimir's." "Where is he?" "Oh, he's in the Ukraine." "Yes, and whose dress is this?" "Well, that is Anna's dress." And so I was able to name all the people in this quilt, even though I had never actually met them. The quilt was tangible evidence of my family's beginnings.

I think that people wonder about my family when they read my books. I have quite a background. My mother's people were Russian and Ukrainian Jews. When they came to this country and finally settled on a little farm in Michigan, they found other countrymen, but not Jews. So there is a whole section of my family that is married to Orthodox Christians. My father's people are Irish. As well as the different nationalities, we also were surrounded with different religious beliefs. My father probably was originally Roman Catholic, but the father I knew all my life was born-again Christian, so imagine the philosophies. I was as comfortable seeing an icon on our wall as I was a mazusa, a menorah, and a shofar. To this day, if you come into my house you will see all of these.

I come from a long line of amazing storytellers. The people from Eastern Europe are, of course, fabulous tellers. My father's people, the Irish, are also fabulous tellers. When you are raised by all these people who tell stories you know you're going to tell stories too. When I was little, my grandmother, the ultimate storyteller, would come, and she'd tell some of her stories a thousand times. Whenever my grandmother would finish, my brother and I would lean into her and say, "Now Bubby, that story you just told, is it a true story?" She'd look at us and tell us that of course it is a true story, but it may not have happened. Of course all stories are true, it doesn't matter whether they happened or not. The wonder of storytelling is read in the faces of the listeners.

I once saw a quote that said all authors and tellers are great liars, because how else could you hope to caress the truth? History is true, but there is also truth in storytelling. My babushka was not only a great teller, she was the one who showed us great miracles every day. These miracles happen in perfectly ordinary places and that's what makes them miracles. I remember watching her cook in the kitchen, because that was her domain. I was always fascinated to watch her. If she had a bottle of vanilla, for example, she'd unscrew it, and if she didn't think anyone was looking, she'd tip it over and pour some on herself so she always smelled delicious.

I wasn't aware that my grandmother was becoming ill. I remember as a child that she didn't put her babushka on her head anymore, and I remember that she didn't dress anymore, and then I remember that it was hard for her to get from her bed to a little chair by the window.

In Michigan during the summers it is quite customary in a very hot spell to go and lie down in the yard at night. I remember that one summer night my brother and I were spread out on a blanket, and suddenly there was my grandmother. She came out of the door in her flannel, of all things. She lay down that night with us, took both our hands, and asked us to look at the stars, so we did. She said, "Do you know what they are?" We said that we knew they were stars, and she said, "No, those are holes and that is heaven showing from the other side. Now I tell you I am going to have to let go, and this is where I go, but when I leave, you will always walk in light." And sure enough she did leave. I was alone in the room with her when she passed. I remember as a child having a sense of what an awesomely beautiful thing I was witnessing because she died with dignity and with grace. I remember watching her for the longest time to see if I could see something move up from her.

After my grandmother's passing, there was a time of great emptiness in my life, and my family chose to sell the farm and move from Michigan to Oakland, California. That is where I met our neighbors, the Washingtons, who eventually became like a second family to me. The first person I met was Stewart. I heard a knock on my front door one day, I went to the door and there was an African American lad. In those days he was all elbows and Adam's apple. He had a paper basket full of flowers in his hands and he said, "Hey, want to buy a May basket?" I told him that it wasn't May and that those were flowers out of our yard. And he smiled and told me that, yes, they were. I knew then he was my kind of guy. I snapped him in the house and we made more paper baskets and went around and pilfered just about everybody's flowers and sold them back to them, too. Stewart has been my best friend now for 37 years. I love and adore this person and have learned so much from him and his entire family.

In the wonderful neighborhood that I live in, the people come in as many colors, philosophies, and ideas as I think there are people on the planet. I remember the day Stewart took me home and I first clapped my eyes on Eula May Walker, his grandma. I had been asking God to give me a sign that my own grandmother was all right and right there in the kitchen I saw Eula take a bottle of vanilla, open it, and put it to her wrist, and I knew then that grandmothers come exactly the same. She used to take us out on the front porch that she called the "talk" porch, and this was where we would sit and tell tales. I heard wonderful stuff from the bayous of Louisiana. You could literally hear the katydids and frogs when she began, and there we were right in the middle of a huge city.

Another wonderful thing about knowing Stewart has been an opportunity to share customs. His family spoke standard English, but when they had reunions and were together they would "slide" into dialect. It was such an honor for me to be a part of these gatherings, that they loved me and trusted me and that I was welcome. Stewart would then come to my house to celebrate Hanukkah and we would light the menorah.

We had other neighbors like the Martinez family. Tomas was the father, and there was Mrs. Martinez (we never called her by her first name—it just wasn't done). At Christmas, they and their five children celebrated Posadas, a time when you go around as Mary and Joseph asking for room at the inn.

I was allowed to have Christmas with Stewart's family at Aunt Lacy and Uncle Bike's home on Ashby Avenue in Berkeley. Uncle Bike was quite a piece of work. He was a mysterious man, gloriously tall and handsome. He had a leg that would come off, and he convinced us—Stewart, Winnie, and me—that all black men, once they were 40, could remove one of their legs. We watched black men's legs for years. Uncle Bike was a wonderful storyteller. He would tip his chair back from the table and start to tell tales, and Aunt Lacy would come into the room and say, "In the face of God, why are you saying things like this to these children?" And she'd say, "Drop the silverware, the Lord is going to strike him with lightning. You just drop everything metal and you pull back from that table because he is going to get hit!" Then Uncle Bike would sit back and just laugh.

I remember the first Christmas I had with Stewart's family, because one of the light bulbs shorted out on the Christmas tree and it started to smoke, and caught the tree on fire. Uncle Bike leaped up at that tree, and out the door it went in a pyrotechnic arc. It landed in the side yard, and all of the children exploded out of the house and danced around the burning tree. I thought, we Jews have a menorah but Baptists light whole trees! This isn't bad!

Knowing and loving Stewart and his family has taught me probably more about the horror of racism in this country than any academic study that I have undertaken. We've shared so much together as families. We've had graduations, we've had babies, we've done weddings, and we've buried our dead together. It is at these moments of crowning life experiences that you're given the opportunity to see why people do what they do within a culture. This is why I think it is important to have authentic voices in literature, because not every child is lucky enough to grow up in the neighborhood like the one where I grew up. They may not know experiences like the ones I have had, but they can experience them secondhand through a book. If the voice is authentic, they are going to get a real, genuine experience. It is these authentic voices that will pull children out of the darkness of confusion and misapprehension and misinformation about each other. I think that if we have a mission at all, that is what we must do.

In our family, the keeping quilt is often used on ceremonial occasions such as weddings and baby namings. The most recent duty the keeping quilt had in our family, was during the loss of my nephew in a terrible accident just two months ago. My dear friend, Stewart, and I always come together at these times, even though we live apart now and the miles separate us. We put the keeping quilt over Brocie's coffin and we mourned. After a death, many Jewish families do what is called sitting shiva, which means you cover all of the mirrors because to see your image in a mirror is vanity. You do not wear shoes, because this shows prosperity and a preoccupation with wealth and possessions. You rent and tear your clothes, you put ashes on your forehead, and you sit and mourn the dead person. When I have been to a funeral with Stewart, there is a much more open type of mourning, and this brought about a discussion between us because for the longest time I held the pain of my nephew's death inside me. I went through the ritual of mourning, but not in the way the women in Stewart's family would have done. They would "fall out" (or faint), which is a wonderful custom that gives you the freedom of really mourning.

During this time Stewart and I had time to talk about our childhood together and ask the things that we had always wondered about each other. After all these years, Stewart asked me if I realized that when he was a little boy that he had never opened a book and seen someone that looked like him. I was stunned—in my arrogance, totally stunned. He also brought to my attention that every morning when he gets up and looks at himself in the mirror, he knows that at least once that day someone will make an issue of his race or he will make an issue of it. I never thought of this.

One thing that happens in my family at Rosh Hashana is the custom of bringing in the new year by dipping a piece of apple in honey and tasting it. Then we talk about how the new year is going to bring sweetness. In my family, though, we also put a book in the youngest family member's hands. Honey is put on the cover, and the child is asked to taste the honey. The family asks the child how it tastes, and the child responds that it is sweet. The family responds that knowledge is sweet and that it is like the bee who made the honey: you have to chase it through the pages of a book. For me, though, this was a promise that was not to come easily because you are also looking at a learning-disabled student who could not read until I was fourteen years old. So you can imagine that the librarians and teachers in my life are the heroes. My English teacher pulled me out of total darkness at the age of fourteen. He is truly my hero, and we are still friends even after thirty years.

If I have any message at all, it certainly is diversity and the celebration of differences. At the same time, my blessings and my thanks go out to people like you who are on the front lines every single day. You dedicate your lives to enlightening and inspiring children, who are, of course, the greatest natural resource of this country and of the world. You spend more hours with our children than we do as parents, and of course you are underpaid, underthanked, and always the first ones to take the flack if something goes wrong. So please, if it is the last thing I do today, allow me to thank you for being here, for choosing the life that you have chosen. I would even argue that it has chosen you.

God bless you. God bless you for being here. I'll say a prayer that my grandmother used to say to me before she would adjourn after we had memorized and talked about these patterns on this keeping quilt. She would lean in and kiss me here and here and she'd say, "I kiss your eyes, I hold your heart in my good keeping, and I am going to thank God this night that I walk the earth with you." I thank God that

I walk the earth with the likes of Virginia Hamilton, Arnold Adoff, James Ransome, Jacqueline Woodson, and all of you. God bless. God bless.

BOOKS BY PATRICIA POLACCO

Writer and illustrator

Meteor! New York: Dodd, 1987.

Boatride with Lillian Two Blossom. New York: Philomel, 1988.

Casey at the Bat. Adapted by Patricia Polacco. New York: Putnam, 1988.

The Keeping Quilt. New York: Simon & Schuster, 1988.

Rechenka's Eggs. New York: Philomel, 1988.

Uncle Vova's Tree. New York: Philomel, 1989.

Babushka's Doll. New York: Simon & Schuster, 1990.

Just Plain Fancy. New York: Bantam, 1990.

Thunder Cake. New York: Philomel, 1990.

Applemando's Dreams. New York: Philomel, 1991.

Some Birthday! New York: Simon & Schuster, 1991.

Chicken Sunday. New York: Philomel, 1992.

Mrs. Katz and Tush. New York: Bantam, 1992.

Picnic at Mudsock Meadow. New York: Putnam, 1992.

Babushka Baba Yaga. New York: Philomel, 1993.

The Bee Tree. New York: Putnam, 1993.

My Rotten, Redheaded, Older Brother. New York: Simon & Schuster, 1994.

Pink and Say. New York: Philomel, 1994.

Tikvah Means Hope. New York: Doubleday, 1994.

Babushka's Mother Goose. New York: Philomel, 1995.

My Ol' Man. New York: Philomel, 1995.

Aunt Chip and the Great Triple Creek Dam Affair. New York: Philomel, 1996.

I Can Hear the Sun. New York: Philomel, 1996.

The Trees of the Dancing Goats. New York: Simon & Schuster, 1996.

Autobiography

Firetalking. New York: Richard C. Owen, 1994.

ABOUT PATRICIA POLACCO

Throughout her publishing career, Patricia Polacco, author and illustrator, has explored themes of hope and tolerance in books that focus on the experiences of characters with various racial, ethnic, and religious affiliations. Born in Lansing, Michigan, to parents of Russian and Ukrainian descent on one side of the family and Irish on the other, she grew up in Oakland, California, in a family of storytellers. She earned an M.F.A. degree in painting from Monash University in Melbourne, Australia, and a Ph.D. in Russian and Greek iconographic history from the Royal Melbourne Institute of Technology. Her many honors include the Sydney Taylor Book Award for *The Keeping Quilt*, the International Reading Association Children's Book Award for *Rechenka's Eggs*, the Commonwealth Club of California Silver Medal for *Babushka's Doll*, the Golden Kite Award for *Chicken Sunday*, and the Educators for Social Responsibility Award.

This chapter is adapted from the presentation Patricia Polacco made as a featured speaker at the twelfth Virginia Hamilton Conference on April 12, 1996.

Uncle Jed's Barbershop by Margaree King Mitchell, illustrated by James Ransome.

10

AUNTS, UNCLES, QUILTS, A SPOTTED DOG AND FLOWERS

JAMES RANSOME

I WAS BORN in North Carolina in a small town called Rich Square, where we lived for about fifteen years until my grandmother decided she didn't want to keep a household any longer. I then moved to Bergenfield, New Jersey, and lived with my mother. I had always loved comic books and drawing as a child, but when I went to Bergenfield High School, where they actually had art programs, I began to immerse myself in the arts. At first, I was interested in filmmaking. I made films until I reached the point where I got tired of asking my friends (and they got tired of being asked) to stay after school to appear in the films. Then I began to animate my own films and this brought me back to drawing and painting which I really love.

I convinced myself that I was going to make a living as an artist no matter what people had said in the past, and people had said a lot in the past, especially when I was living in that small town in North Carolina. People said that there was no possibility of making a living or surviving as an artist. That has always been in my mind, so once I got to high school in New Jersey, I worked very hard to make succeeding as an artist a real possibility.

There were many and varied influences in my life, including *Mad* magazine. As a child I actually imitated the format of *Mad* magazine and used it to make up stories about me and my friends having different adventures as we got older. Also, comic books were a big influence, as they are for most kids, especially those who live far away from big cities and don't get a chance to see museums and galleries. Comic books were the first images of art that I saw, and I began copying them. Once I went to art school, I fell in love with painters such as Mary Cassatt. I especially love her patterns, the relationship she has between the people and the way she lays the paint down. I also liked the work of Winslow Homer, one of the few artists of his time who painted African Americans or people of African descent with a sense of dignity. Another influence has been a Spanish painter, Sorolla. He paints very loose, and I love the way he lays the paint down. I also enjoy his strong rich colors. And then there is John Singer Sargent. Most people know his portraits but I love his outdoor paintings. He paints in light and he paints these figures with light filtering through the trees. One of my favorite paintings is called "The Hermit." These are the types of painters and paintings that really inspire me.

In art school I became interested in sports paintings, and I decided that I wanted to work with *Sports Illustrated*. I also wanted to do posters, calendars, and anything dealing with sports. During my senior year, I did a sports painting that was used on a calendar that Citibank put together. After I graduated they eventually bought the painting from me. I was also interested in the Society of Illustrators. They have an annual scholarship competition for college students, and my piece was used on the cover of the catalog. It was also used on a greeting card and even led to shopping bags and one of those shopping bags was made into a jigsaw puzzle.

About this time I saw a book illustrated by Jerry Pinkney called *The Patchwork Quilt*. Children's books began to become a focus for me, and I painted three images of a little girl to show art directors that I could paint children. These images went into my portfolio, and they led to the illustrations in my first picture book *Do Like Kyla*. It's about a little sister who imitates her big sister, and then the role is reversed. This was the best assignment I had been involved in since graduation. I enjoyed working on what I considered a series of paintings and taking these two characters and developing them. After this, I began to show my artwork to other publishing companies. The next art project I became involved in was *How Many Stars in the Sky?*, about a young boy and his father trying to count all the stars in the sky in one night while Mama is away. Next came *Aunt Flossie's Hats (and Crab Cakes Later)*, the story of Susan and Sara visiting with Aunt Flossie, on Sundays where they share tea, cookies, crab cakes, and stories about the hats in a hat collection. This was followed by *All the Lights in the Night*, which tells of Benjamin and Moses making a dangerous journey to Palestine and their celebration of Hanukkah along the way. I was offered an opportunity to illustrate a book jacket for *Winning Scheherazade* which is based on the Arabian Nights tales of Scheherazade the storyteller.

Other book jackets I've illustrated include *Middle of Somewhere*, a story of a girl living in South Africa; *Chevrolet Saturdays*, about a boy and the relationship he has with his stepfather; *The Cry of the Wolf*, a story of a man hunting the last wolf in England; *Down in the Piney Woods*, the story of a girl living in the South in the late 1950s, and then the sequel entitled *Moriah's Pond*. I've also done a reissue of *Sounder* in soft cover and the covers of an eight-book series which began with *Ziggy and the Black Dinosaurs*. This series is about Ziggy and his three friends, who are African American boys with very different personalities. They discover things about African American history on their different journeys.

Other books I've illustrated include *Red Dancing Shoes*, the story about a girl who gets a pair of shoes from her grandmother and dances through the town to show them off to everyone she knows. Another is *The Girl Who Wore Snakes*, the story about Ali, who loves snakes. Then there was *The Hummingbird Garden*, about a lady who has a beautiful garden that attracts hummingbirds. The story tells how the lady eventually befriends a little girl.

My favorite book I've illustrated is *Uncle Jed's Barbershop*. This is a story about Uncle Jed, the only black barber in the county, who is saving up money to open his own barbershop. There is an interesting footnote to this story because the writer did not know that my father was a barber and had always wanted to open his own barbershop. The year that I received this story to illustrate, my father was finally able to open his own shop. Also interesting to the background of this book is that the writer and I had never met when I painted the book. Afterwards, when we did meet, she mentioned that the picture of a house in the book looked so much like the farm she grew up on in Mississippi. This is amazing because I based that illustration on a house where we used to have our family reunions down in North Carolina, where I grew up. The chicken coop in the background is from my grandfather's house, and so are the chickens. Whenever I go down to see him, I take tons of pictures of his chickens in case I want to use them in future projects.

Uncle Jed's Barbershop opens as Uncle Jed tells Sarah Jean, his favorite niece, how one day he wants to open a barbershop and about how big it is going to be. As the story unfolds, Sarah Jean becomes sick and has to be taken to the hospital, where the family discovers that she needs an operation. They have to borrow the money from Uncle Jed, so he has to postpone opening his barbershop. A few years later, Uncle Jed has managed to save three thousand dollars and he is ready to open his barbershop, when he gets the news that the Great Depression has begun and the banks have lost all of his money. He has to start saving all over again. When Uncle Jed hears of the bank failing, an illustration depicts him sitting next to his brother. The model for the brother is my friend and mentor, Jerry Pinkney. I met

Jerry when I was in school because I knew his son, Scott Pinkney, who is now an art director in Canada. When I began working on *Do Like Kyla,* my first book, I called Jerry and asked him if I could come and talk to him about the project. I have been visiting with him and his wife Gloria ever since. (*Uncle Jed's Barbershop* is dedicated to Jerry and Gloria Pinkney).

Uncle Jed continues to cut hair. Most people can't afford to pay him, so they give him food, but finally, after years of saving, his dream comes true and he opens his barbershop. People come from all over to get their hair cut. Unfortunately, Uncle Jed is very old now and doesn't live much longer. He passes away after opening his barbershop, but he has lived to see his dream come true. The fall leaves in the story are symbols—symbols of hope, symbols of change. Just as the leaves in the fall are dying, so is Uncle Jed. I like to use symbolic images in my books. I always try to go a little bit beyond what's on the surface, hoping that the viewer can read into these things, if not consciously, then subconsciously.

Then there is *The Creation*, the winner of the Coretta Scott King Award for illustration in 1995. This is a story written by James Weldon Johnson in the 1920s. In this book, I decided it would be best to have a storyteller telling the story to a group of children. Imagine that this story was told to him as a child, and now he's telling it to another group of children. When they grow up, they will tell it to another group of children. The storyteller tells them how God stepped out of the darkness and created the heavens and the earth.

Celie and the Harvest Fiddler is a story about a African American girl living in the South in the 1870s, who wants to win the costume contest at the All Hallows' Eve harvest festival, and the problems she has when she meets a fiddler who has magical powers. *My Best Shoes* features children talking about their favorite pair of shoes for each day of the week, from sturdy lace-up shoes to naked feet to toe shoes. *Bonesy and Isabel* features the story of a girl, Isabel, who is adopted from El Salvador and comes to live on a farm with many animals. She quickly learns about the love and caring the family feels for each other on this farm. She becomes friendly with an old dog named Bonesy and she must deal with her grief when he dies.

Another title is *Freedom's Fruit*, which is a story that begins on the endpapers with cats coming towards us. They take us directly to Mama Marina's house where a slave owner is coming in because he wants her to put a spell on the grapes to keep the slaves from eating them. Mama Marina, a slave woman and conjurer in the Old South, does this for a small fee, with hopes of buying the freedom of her daughter, Sheba. When Sheba comes home, she is upset because of the spell on the grapes. Mama Marina tells her that she wishes for her to be free, but the daughter won't leave without her boyfriend. (For all of those who wonder if my children appear in my books, my oldest daughter is in the lady's arms in one of the illustrations. This is the first book that she has appeared in.) It is soon discovered that the slave owner plans to hire out the boyfriend, and everyone is upset, so Mama Marina puts a different spell on the grapes. This time she gives the grapes to her daughter and the boyfriend, and when they eat them they become very sick, very old, and very weak. Mama Marina tells them that this was in her plan and everything is going to be fine. She is then able to buy the two of them at a very cheap price because they are so old and so weak. She puts Sheba and her boyfriend on a wagon, and they ride off as the spell slowly starts wearing off. Mama Marina is able to watch them as they roll away toward freedom.

Then there is *Sweet Clara and the Freedom Quilt,* which I will use as an example of how I illustrate a book. First, I begin with research. I visit libraries and bookstores, and with this particular book, I felt a lot of pressure to be correct because it is about slavery. I didn't want to make any mistakes, so I read and looked at pictures of slaves to see how they dressed. I went to Colonial Williamsburg and to Carter's Grove Plantation to do research. The slave owner's house at Carter's Grove has been changed a lot since the 1800s because the family continued living there until the 1930s. I went to the slave quarters and went on a tour there, and only then did I begin to get an understanding of how slaves lived.

After talking to family members, I discovered that the plantation my family came from is not too far from where I grew up in North Carolina. It was called the Verona Plantation. I used the Verona Plantation in the first picture you see in *Sweet Clara and the Freedom Quilt.* It's a portrait of the plantation, the way it may have looked back in the 1800s. It was owned by General Matt and Patty Ransome, and this book is dedicated to the first slave they brought to this plantation and named Emma Ransome. This house is also used in the book *Freedom's Fruit.* The slave owner lives in that house on Verona Plantation.

After the research, when I go back to my studio, I begin working on the dummy book, using very loose, simple sketches. Then I ask people to model for me. My models are usually friends and family members who come over to my studio and dress in different costumes. I photograph them acting out the different scenes. I then draw these scenes on paper and send those drawings to my art director, who usually sends them back with some small comments and I make the necessary adjustments. Then I begin painting.

First I put a wash of color on top of the drawings, so that I can see my colors much better once I start painting. And then I do all the faces first on all the pages. Then I pull out individual paintings and work on them until I complete them, first painting in the background, then each individual character, working my way across the page until they are finally completed. The very last thing that I did in *Sweet Clara and the Freedom Quilt* was the pattern on the quilt.

Sweet Clara and the Freedom Quilt is the story of a girl named Clara, who is sold from one plantation to another. Clara doesn't like working out in the fields. When her Aunt Rachel (who is not really her aunt) teaches her how to sew, Clara gets a job in the big house. There she learns about the Underground Railroad and freedom up North. She then decides to make a quilt that is really a map toward this freedom. When she makes her escape, she leaves the quilt behind with Aunt Rachel. Aunt Rachel then shares the quilt with others so that they can escape. While Clara and young Jack run for freedom, they stop for Clara's mother, and she joins them on their quest following the Underground Railroad.

Other projects I've worked on include *Home*, a collaboration between writers and illustrators to raise money for the homeless. Writers wrote about different, favorite places of a home, and illustrators were asked to bring those places to life through art. I contributed a painting of a closet. The following year, I was asked to be a part of *Speak,* which was composed of children's book artists writing about their dogs. I painted a picture of my dalmation, Clinton, and my wife wrote a poem about him. It is now even available as a greeting card. Both the book and the greeting card help raise money for animal shelters. Another project was an African American storytelling mural for the Children's Museum in Indianapolis. The mural features an African in the background telling stories, and a man from the South, a sharecropper, and a contemporary grandmother in the center telling a story to a group of children. For the mural I created a 60-inch by 40-inch painting in my studio, and the museum blew it up to eight feet high by sixteen feet long.

I live and work in Poughkeepsie, New York, in a house that used to belong to a doctor. We converted his office into my studio. There is a room that I call my drawing room, which has several drawing desks in it. There's a light box and lots of books that I use to help me create new books. There is a hallway that I keep my artwork in when it is not on exhibit. From time to time, museums, galleries, and even schools call me and want to borrow the paintings. In one of the former examining rooms is my studio, where I do most of the painting, I have taken a wall down and expanded two rooms into one. I have an easel here, and the works of my favorite illustrators and painters fill the walls and inspire me as I work. None of my work hangs in this room. I have some of my daughter Jaime's work in this room, though.

Sharing how I develop the images for my books and encouraging children to read, write, and create their own stories are the reasons that I illustrate books. To see young people brimming with questions, thoughts, and ideas based on a book that I have illustrated lets me know that I have made a major contribution to their lifelong love of literature and art.

BOOKS BY JAMES RANSOME

Illustrator

Aunt Flossie's Hats (and Crab Cakes Later). Written by Elizabeth Howard. New York: Clarion, 1990.

Do Like Kyla. Written by Angela Johnson. New York: Orchard, 1990.

All the Lights in the Night. Written by Arthur Levine. New York: Morrow, 1991.

How Many Stars in the Sky? Written by Lenny Hort. New York: Morrow, 1991.

The Girl Who Wore Snakes. Written by Angela Johnson. New York: Orchard, 1993.

The Hummingbird Garden. Written by Christine Widman. New York: Macmillan, 1993.

Red Dancing Shoes. Written by Denise L. Patrick. New York: Morrow, 1993.

Sweet Clara and the Freedom Quilt. Written by Deborah Hopkinson. New York: Knopf, 1993.

Uncle Jed's Barbershop. Written by Margaree King Mitchell. New York: Simon & Schuster, 1993.

Bonesy and Isabel. Written by Michael J. Rosen. New York: Harcourt, 1994.

The Creation. Written by James Weldon Johnson. New York: Holiday House, 1994.

My Best Shoes. Written by Marilee Robin Burton. New York: Morrow, 1994.

That Cat! Written by Eve B. Feldman. New York: Morrow, 1994.

Ziggy and the Black Dinosaurs. Written by Sharon M. Draper. East Orange, NJ: Just Us Books, 1994.

Celie and the Harvest Fiddler. Written by Vanessa and Valerie Flournoy. New York: Morrow, 1995.

Dark Day, Light Night. Written by Jan Carr. New York: Hyperion, 1995.

The Old Dog. Written by Charlotte Zolotow. New York: HarperCollins, 1995.

Bimmi Finds a Cat. Written by Elisabeth J. Stewart. New York: Clarion, 1996.

Eli and the Swamp Man. Written by Charlotte Watson Sherman. New York: HarperCollins, 1996.

Freedom's Fruit. Written by William H. Hooks. New York: Random House, 1996.

The Wagon. Written by Tony Johnston. New York: Morrow, 1996.

Illustrator of book jackets

The Middle of Somewhere: A Story of South Africa. Written by Sheila Gordon. New York: Orchard, 1990.

Winning Scheherazade. Written by Judith Gorog. New York: Atheneum, 1991.

Children of the Fire. Written by Harriet G. Robinet. New York: Atheneum, 1992.

The Cry of the Wolf. Written by Melvin Burgess. New York: Morrow, 1992.

Down in the Piney Woods. Written by Ethel Footman Smothers. New York: Knopf, 1992.

Chevrolet Saturdays. Written by Candy Dawson Boyd. New York: Macmillan, 1993.

Harriet: The Life and World of Harriet Beecher Stowe. Written by Norma Johnston. New York: Four Winds, 1994.

Moriah's Pond. Written by Ethel Footman Smothers. New York: Knopf, 1995.

Sounder. Written by William H. Armstrong. New York: HarperCollins, 1995.

Included in collaborations

Home: A Collaboration of Thirty Distinguished Authors and Illustrators to Aid the Homeless. Edited by Michael J. Rosen. New York: HarperCollins, 1992.

Speak! Children's Book Illustrators Brag about Their Dogs. Edited by Michael J. Rosen. New York: Harcourt, 1993.

ABOUT JAMES RANSOME

James Ransome earned his degree in illustration from Pratt Institute in Brooklyn, New York. Using design, perspective, and choice of palette, he displays his talent as a visual storyteller by bringing out the special voice of each book he illustrates. He is currently a Society of

Illustrators member and has exhibited paintings in many group and solo shows. He won the Coretta Scott King Award for illustrating James Weldon Johnson's *The Creation* and received a Coretta Scott King Honor for *Uncle Jed's Barbershop* by Margaree King Mitchell. Both books were also American Library Association Notable Children's Books. James Ransome has said of his work that "by conveying to young readers the individual traits of characters I only hope that I am instilling an appreciation for the wonderfully unique qualities and cultural and racial differences we all possess." Mr. Ransome currently lives in Poughkeepsie, New York, with his wife, Lesa, their daughters Jaime and Maya, and their dalmation, Clinton.

This chapter is adapted from the slide presentation James Ransome made as a featured speaker at the twelfth Virginia Hamilton Conference on April 12, 1996.

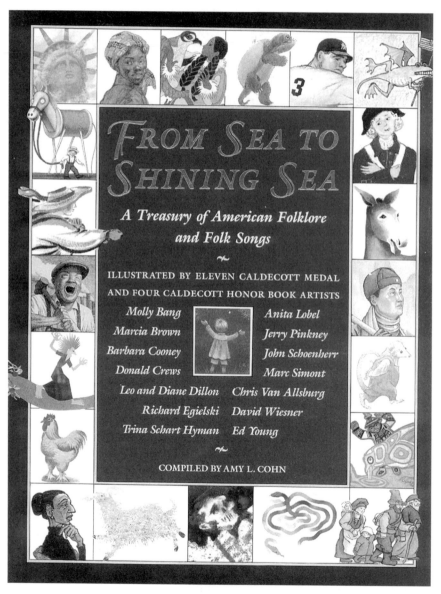

From Sea to Shining Sea: A Treasury of American Folklore and Folk Songs. By Amy Cohn, illustrated by eleven Caldecott Medal and four Caldecott Honor Book artists.

11

I HEAR AMERICA SINGING
AN EDITOR'S POINT OF VIEW
DIANNE HESS

CREATING QUALITY multicultural books, for me, has been a continuing thrill and a challenge. Facing the twenty-first century with America's rapidly changing demographics is indeed exciting, as doors open wide to us as publishers—enabling us to explore new worlds and to discover the rich heritages that belong to us all. America is different from any other country in the world. We exist on an enormous expanse of land that is large enough to contain many sizable countries. And although there are people of every culture and every race living here, we all call ourselves Americans.

Here, in this vast land, we have only one "official" language. We have one system of money. We share one central government. And we can travel to nearly any major city in the world and expect that people will communicate with us in our own language.

As an American, I am always surprised when I travel through Europe, how within a space the size of the U.S., you can enter into different countries in the time it would take to drive from one state to the next. Germany alone borders on eight countries! Imagine driving from New York to New Jersey, or from Texas to neighboring Louisiana and crossing over a state line and having to show your passport (although that has recently changed in Europe). Imagine driving from California into Oregon and having to change money, speak a different language, and adjust to an entirely different culture. Imagine if national television meant a TV station covering only Ohio, or West Virginia, or Idaho.

There is an amazing analogy to be drawn from the European borders which lead from one country to the next. They illustrate how America once was when it was inhabited solely by the Indian nations. For North America alone, including what is now Canada, Alaska, and the contiguous U.S., was inhabited by an estimated seven million people of more than a thousand nations, who spoke hundreds of different languages and had their own distinct cultures. What I wouldn't give to be able to travel back in time and visit the Americas that existed then!

We were a multicultural place then, and we are one now. Having one language, one money system, one government, and national TV stations sometimes makes us think that we are all one culture. But our culture consists of people of many nations within each of the 52 states. Somehow, the cultures of America defy borders.

While walking down the street in my New York City neighborhood, it is conceivable that in less than one hour, I might pass American citizens who are either from—or descendants of—Jamaica, Haiti, East India, Nigeria, Kenya, Puerto Rico, the Dominican Republic, Cuba, Colombia, Japan, China, Korea, Israel, Egypt, Italy, Ireland, Germany, Great Britain, Russia, Greece, or Ukraine, to name only a few places. If all of these people are Americans—then what, exactly, is our identity? What is it that makes us all one people?

These are the questions that our foreparents asked after the American Revolution, after we had broken away from Europe. Americans, who are by nature a mixture of nationalities, have always been looking to discover a national identity. When our earliest architects hoped to develop a uniquely American style of buildings, they still borrowed heavily from Europe. The nation's capitol was filled with monuments that were in the image of Greek and Roman temples, with elaborate scrolls and columns and domes. Many churches were modeled after Italian cathedrals. There was even a time when an artist was commissioned to create a sculpture of our first president, and using sculptures of the larger-than-life Greek gods as his model, built an enormous nude version of George Washington, wearing only a fig leaf! Somehow, that wasn't what the old patriarchs had in mind for the image of an American president.

Today, sitting in my office, while making decisions about which books to publish, I ask myself these same questions about the identity of America. And the more multicultural books I publish, which represent facets of our culture, the more I begin to discover pieces to that vast puzzle of who we are.

Every day, I feel very fortunate to be in a position to help American children of every background to discover and embrace their unique cultural heritages. And every day, I try to discover fresh new American voices of the multi-nationed people who call America "home."

Scholastic Press and the Blue Sky Press have made a firm commitment to publishing the diverse voices of America. Virginia Hamilton, Leo and Diane Dillon, Walter Dean Myers, Shonto Begay, Lulu

Delacre, Floyd Cooper, Pat McKissack, Jacqueline Woodson, Joyce Hansen, Laurence Yep, Ed Young, Amy L. Cohn, Fran Manushkin, Jan Spivey Gilchrist, Gary Soto, Brian Pinkney—this is just a sampling of the authors and artists that grace the Scholastic lists.

Besides our commitment to diversity and high quality, Scholastic has a credo. It is given to every new employee. And when we moved to our new offices a year and a half ago, the Scholastic credo was woven into the carpets and placed in the center of all twelve floors—through the heart of the company. As we walk through the halls, it reminds us every day of our most important and sacred goals: to present children with the best possible materials that reflect all the best in human values; to have an awareness and respect for all people and their various cultures, whatever they may be; to be respectful of the environment; and to pass along a love of knowledge to future generations.

These are the values with which we hope to infuse every Scholastic book, and the gifts that we hope to give to every child in America. And we make every effort to create books for each and every child to reflect an America of which they can feel a part.

And now I would like to describe some of these books. There are a number of editors, including myself, at Scholastic who contribute books to our hardcover lines. And out of the roughly 60 books per year which we publish, one-third are multicultural. Since my own books are the ones that I know best, I will focus only on the multicultural titles I have published, rather than look at our entire list.

My intent is to illustrate how the many voices of America are a reflection of the world. I hope that these books will touch young readers today and help them to discover their own American voices.

From Sea to Shining Sea: A Treasury of American Folklore and Folksongs Compiled by Amy L. Cohn. Illustrated by eleven Caldecott Medal artists and four Caldecott Honor Book artists. Here is a history of America told in chronological order through folklore and folk songs. Beginning with the stories and songs of Native Americans and continuing on with the folklore of the first settlers on the continent, the Revolutionary War, westward expansion, the development of the waterways, the era of slavery, the development of the railroad, and folklore from the twentieth century, this collection is perhaps the best example of how our history and literature grew from a mixture of world cultures. Indexes by culture, geographical region, song type, and tale type. Historic timeline also included.

The Mud Pony Retold by Caron Lee Cohen. Illustrated by Shonto Begay. A traditional Skidi Pawnee tale of a boy who creates a pony out of mud that comes alive and guides him through his life. The story was adapted from a version by George Dorsey who recorded Pawnee traditions and tales between 1899 and 1902.

Ma'ii and Cousin Horned Toad Retold and illustrated by Shonto Begay. A traditional Navajo trickster tale, told to the author by his grandmother, who lived to be 113 years old.

The Magic of Spider Woman By Lois Duncan. Illustrated by Shonto Begay. A story about the legendary Spider Woman, who brought weaving to the Navajo nation.

Navajo: Visions and Voices from Across the Mesa Art and poetry by Shonto Begay. Pieces of Begay's fine artwork that are displayed in museums throughout the Southwest come together with his poetic narrative. In this work, he perceptively shows contemporary Navajo life in counterpoint to the ever-present ancient world.

Arroz con Leche: Favorite Songs and Rhymes from Latin America Selected and illustrated by Lulu Delacre. A bilingual collection for young children.

Las Navidades: Favorite Christmas Songs from Latin America Selected and illustrated by Lulu Delacre. A bilingual collection of Christmas songs for the family. Arranged chronologically from Christmas Eve to the Epiphany, the book includes descriptions of the traditions associated with each of the twelve songs.

Vejigante: Masquerader Written and illustrated by Lulu Delacre. A picture storybook about a young boy in Puerto Rico, who makes his dream of becoming a Vejigante masquerader come true. Winner of the Américas Book Award.

Golden Tales: Myths, Legends, and Folktales from Latin America Retold and illustrated by Lulu Delacre. (Spanish version: *De Oro y Esmeraldas: Mitos, Leyendas y Cuentos Populares de Latinoamérica*). The story of Latin America told through folklore. Shows how the Indian, African, and European cultures blended to create what we know today as Latin American literature. Annotated with fascinating research notes on the art.

The Bossy Gallito Retold by Lucía M. Gonzaléz. Illustrated by Lulu Delacre. A favorite cumulative nursery rhyme told by a master Cuban American storyteller. Twice named a Pura Belpré Award Honor Book, once for text and once for art.

Señor Cat's Romance and Other Favorite Stories from Latin America Retold by Lucía M. Gonzaléz. Illustrated by Lulu Delacre. A collection of six best-known, best-loved tales from Latin America, including "Juan Bobo and the Three-Legged Pot," "Cucarachita Martina," and "Señor Cat's Romance," retold and illustrated by the award-winning Latin American author/artist team.

Lion Dancer: Ernie Wan's Chinese New Year   By Kate Waters and Madeline Slovenz-Low. Photographs by Martha Cooper. Six-year-old Ernie Wan dances his first Lion Dance on the streets of Chinatown in New York City.

Tapenum's Day: A Wampanoag Indian in Pilgrim Times   By Kate Waters. Photographs by Russ Kendall. A coming of age story of a Wampanoag Indian boy in the 1620s. Companion book to *Sarah Morton's Day: A Day in the Life of a Pilgrim Girl* and *Samuel Eaton's Day: A Day in the Life of a Pilgrim Boy.*

Eskimo Boy: Life in an Inupiaq Eskimo Village   Written and photographed by Russ Kendall. This year in the life of a six-year-old Eskimo boy in Shishmaref, Alaska, shows the blend of the modern world with the ancient world and the profound effect of weather on a culture.

Russian Girl: Life in an Old Russian Town   Written and photographed by Russ Kendall. Focuses on the daily life of a ten-year-old Russian girl, and captures historic moments of perestroika.

Neve Shalom/Wahat Al-Salam Oasis of Peace   By Laurie Dolphin. Photographed by Ben Dolphin. Neve Shalom, the community in Israel that promotes peace between Jews and Arabs, has been nominated four times for a Nobel Peace Prize. This book focuses on two young boys from the Neve Shalom school, who, by learning each other's culture and language, become friends. Winner of the American Jewish Book Award.

Mermaid Tales from Around the World   By Mary Pope Osborne. Illustrated by Troy Howell. Mermaids are strong, independent women. In this collection of twelve tales from around the world, the artist uses the distinctive art style of each culture.

Favorite Greek Myths   By Mary Pope Osborne. Illustrated by Troy Howell. A collection of fourteen classic tales which are at the root of Western literature.

Favorite Norse Myths   By Mary Pope Osborne. Illustrated by Troy Howell. A collection of fourteen classic tales, also at the root of Western literature.

Winter Poems   Selected by Barbara Rogasky. Illustrated by Trina Schart Hyman. A selection of classic poems about winter, which paints a broad portrait of the season. Illustrated with paintings of a multiracial family in a New Hampshire farm community.

The Great Fire   By Jim Murphy. This Newbery Honor Book dramatically depicts the great Chicago fire of 1871, and later discusses how the Irish were targeted as the cause of the fire.

From the Notebooks of Melanin Sun By Jacqueline Woodson. In this Coretta Scott King Honor Award novel, a thirteen-year-old African American boy probes deeply into his own feelings about racism and homosexuality when he discovers that his mother is in a relationship with a white woman.

The Captive By Joyce Hansen. In this Coretta Scott King Honor Award book, Kofi, a young Ashanti nobleman is sold into slavery by the family's own black slave. Sold to a Puritan farmer in Massachusetts, Kofi is finally freed by a free African American shipbuilder who dreams of returning the Africans to their rightful homeland across the sea.

ABOUT THE AUTHOR

Diane Hess is Executive Editor of Scholastic Press. "I Hear America Singing" is adapted from the slide presentation she gave at the eleventh Virginia Hamilton Conference on April 21, 1995.

Black and White by Margaret Wise Brown, illustrated by Charles Shaw.

12

UPDATING THE RACE
TRANSFORMATIONS IN RACIAL PRESENTATION SINCE 1975

OPAL J. MOORE

A really good book or painting concerning blacks or women is as hard to sell now as it ever was. True art is too complex to reflect the party line. Art that tries hard to tell the truth unretouched is difficult and often offensive. It tears down our heroes and heart-warming convictions, violates canons of politeness and humane compromise.

John Gardner, On Moral Fiction[1]

I LIKE JOHN GARDNER, the way he tried to talk, straight from the shoulder, about morality and story. Maybe I like him because he was a white American male artist and teacher talking about morality and art in the turbulent 1970s, when many of his peers were, at best, embarrassed by the conflation of art and truth, and at worst, scornful of it. Yet Gardner insisted upon the message that was "as old as the hills, drawn from Homer, Plato, Aristotle, Dante, and the rest."[2] As old as whoever told Homer his first bedtime stories.

The moral purpose of story was revived in America in the narratives of the captive black African who wrote and told the stories of the enslaved masses, trusting that the truth would cross the fictitious borders of slavery and freedom, permeate the deepest feeling of white humanity, and move us all, white and black, towards a rumored possibility of freedom and self-respect. Since then, the African American artist has believed in the possibility of an art that could save us. This belief instructed the blues, opened the door to jazz, and was the cornerstone of liberation literature in America. Even so, Gardner did not back away from it. He tried to embrace what seemed a contradiction.

I came to the Virginia Hamilton Conference of 1995, twenty years after Mildred D. Taylor was awarded the Newbery for her groundbreaking novel, *Roll of Thunder, Hear My Cry*, to review this history of what seemed a contradiction—the invention of a moral art for the young adult, a story art that would represent the truths of America's racial dilemma, a story meant to "improve our lives, and not debase it."[3] I wanted to ask how the representations of race in literature for young readers had, so far, evolved.

Story art encourages us to trace backwards for an explanation or illumination of a conclusion. Our experiences with story encourage a desire to impose plot upon our unstoried realities, to trace an event back to an initiating action. Artists will tell you that what works for story (first this happens, then something else, then something else...) is unreliable in the areas of history, science, or literary critical enquiry, that the imposition of such organization upon events is the lie in our fictional truths. Still, in 1993, two published works, *The Giver* by Lois Lowry and *The Toning of the Sweep* by Angela Johnson, made me wonder about the state of young adult "race literature."

Two writers signaled the first transformations:

In 1974, Virginia Hamilton received the Newbery Medal and other distinctions for her novel *M.C. Higgins, The Great*. Her *Planet of Junior Brown* had been named a Newbery Honor Book in 1972. *Junior Brown* and *Higgins* anticipated the 1980s in the way that they backgrounded America's racial history. They went on to illuminate the lives of children of various ethnicities and their struggles to negotiate the destructive forces of an alien, distant and illogical adult world.

Taylor took on history. *Roll of Thunder, Hear My Cry* ably instructs the reader in the mechanics of terrorism and its historical role in oppressing black Americans and maintaining white hegemony. The novel narrates the story of a black, southern agrarian family during the 1930s trying to retain the family farm. Their story represents the larger struggle of black people to hold America's feet to her own moral fire, to lay claim to America as homeplace, to identify the knowledge that defines what black people used to mean when we could unhesitatingly refer to "*The* Black Experience," to throw light into the unlit corners of "race relations." Black struggle was not made subtext, but *the* text. Taylor, making the mostly correct assumption that neither black nor white Americans knew enough about the role of race in American history, constructed a multi-faceted story of a black family and placed it squarely inside of the grand American epic; she, in effect, restored several of the excised pages concerning black presence to our mutilated history books.

Appropriately, *Roll of Thunder* employs the features of the epic: the symbol and sweep of the ancestral lands; the spiritual presence of the ancestors; the nobility of the family organization; the explication of the functional mores of the family; and, the accumulation of details that reveal the grand scale of a family's battle to survive, and even to conquer, the cosmic and human forces that challenge its existence. In this way, Taylor brought to an ethnically diverse readership the complexity of black American story. The novel explores the intricate processes that constituted conscious resistance to oppression—the difficulty of maintaining coherence of family, purpose, and vision; of protecting one's humanity; of balancing moral strength against human frailty; of achieving self-definition and self-actualization as the foundation for moral integrity. At a time when integration was beginning to be mistaken for a racial panacea, Taylor's story reminded us of the greater wisdoms that undergirded our black survival.

Compared to Hamilton's lyrical lightness of style and voice, Taylor's novels are blood-filled dramas full of showdowns between the good and the evil. Together, these women writers lifted the black subject out of the realm of Sambo, Kettle-head, Mingo, and "Nigger" Jim.

In my fabricated archeology of the evolution of modern children's literature, the early works of these two novelists offer a couple of Rosetta stones to help interpret the subsequent signs of a moral art in the novels of three decades to follow, and to define the aesthetic criteria for such art.

Novelist Toni Morrison, in her series of essays *Playing in the Dark: Whiteness and the Literary Imagination*, clarifies the tension in the literary world between the aesthetics of truth and revelation in the work of black artists, and the persistent silences on the subject of race in the literary productions of white writers. The idea that the subject of race was, like sex, a subject inappropriate for polite discourse, also ruled the novel:

> ...the habit of ignoring race is understood to be a graceful, even generous liberal gesture. To notice is to recognize an already discredited difference. To enforce its invisibility through silence is to allow the black body a shadowless participation in the dominant cultural body. According to this logic, every well-bred instinct argues against noticing and forecloses adult discourse.[4]

Morrison's observation suggests that the "well bred instinct," carried into literary practice, would necessitate that the black subject be regarded as a multifaceted vulgarity. The images and stories of black people (those uncut by raucous laughter) would be deemed inescapably political and infused with accusation, guilt and didactic historical discourses that would be automatically crippling, if not totally destructive, to the project of Art. If a black character were used in a story, his/her blackness had to be rigorously denied, invalidated, shut down, in order for Art to take place. (Blackness is unruly, liable to get out of hand without warning. Better to avoid it altogether.) "[I]n matters of race," Morrison tells us, "silence and evasion have historically ruled literary discourse."[5]

This evasion in the language is fear.

Dianne Johnson's critical work, *Telling Tales: The Pedagogy and Promise of African American Literature for Youth*, is titled with a double entendre that may recall, for some of us, the euphemism once demanded of children by their parents, in the days when language content was carefully monitored for both social and political reasons. The word *lie* was considered rude, and not to be spoken by children; its use was frowned upon by adults. Of course euphemisms themselves are lies that "tell." Johnson admonishes the adults who influence the reading habits of children that "we ...must be concerned about the messages that are encoded in African American children's literature. What are we telling our youth, how are we communicating that which we tell them, and what are the implications of what we tell them?"[6]

Johnson's discussion could draw upon Morrison's observations regarding the workings of silences. *Telling Tales* recalls, at once, a timidity of language that would be rejected during the Black Power movement of the 1960s, and the empowering act of telling one's own story—telling the tale. Both Hamilton and Taylor were seeking ways to reject the careful silences that once characterized the "black" telling of our tales. The dismantling of carefully structured silences was both liberating and heavy with responsibility—to do the story justice, to tell it right. Their work would open the door for Walter Dean Myers, Julius Lester, Joyce Hansen, Rosa Guy, and Angela Johnson. These writers would begin to create a "true art" that attempts to tell the unretouched stories of life in America, shattering beloved icons and myths as they wrote, violating canons of politeness and compromise.

The problem with truth is its disruptiveness, the way it upsets established structures of thought, challenges faith. Critic Isabelle Jan, conceding the role of children's literature as socializing tool, advocates providing children with "tales which have a social or political implication and help the child to adapt to his background by providing codes of behavior as well as a national mythology."[7] Johnson notes that "the critic must recognize that there is not, definitively, one national mythology."[8]

If children's books are conceived as socializing tools, the question is, which myths to tell, which set of codes to endorse? For the black writer whose collective racial story is one of betrayal, the myth of democracy is not valuable to the goal of helping a child "adapt to his background." For the white writer, no matter how marginalized his personal history, the myth of America as the land of opportunity for all is the bright and shining promise in Lady Liberty's torch. Each story has some "truth," but moral story, as Gardner stipulates, is in the total effect of the art, not in its parts. In the traditional debate, each writer claims the truth of his own portion, denying the truth of the other. Or, even if each writer offers sympathy for the other's point of view, it is not enough. Neither pity nor reparations will serve. Nothing less than "becoming" the other, for the sake of the art, will suffice.

The question of *which* myths to tell has seldom been explored in an effective way. The argument is frequently constructed according to notions of "good art" vs. "bad art," i.e., "imaginative" art vs. "didactic" messages, "Art for Art's sake" vs. "functional Art." The accusation leveled by white critics regarding the art of black writers was often, "Your message is showing!" The retort of black artists and critics regarding the work of white artists was often, "Your racist lie is showing." This debate is perhaps most famously captured in the "friendly exchange of letters" between *New York Times* children's book editor George Woods and writer/critic, Julius Lester.

Lester took issue with two statements in George Woods's review of December 7, 1969, in which the editor admitted: "...I don't like the so-called books for blacks.... They have merit; they're an attempt to right a long-standing injustice, but it's a stampede that has produced words and pictures without heart, without soul." Woods went on to offer the opinion that "The best books in this area are about blacks and for whites. The whites are the ones who need to know the condition of their fellow humans. The Negro knows his condition. It is the white who must be brought to sympathy and understanding."[9]

Lester rejected Woods's idea that black people cannot or should not learn anything about themselves, pursuing a different argument: "When it comes to books by and about blacks, you need new standards with which to evaluate them."[10] In so saying, he seemed to hint at some fundamentally different aesthetic at work in books for blacks when the differences are in the *which*. Which national myth, which codes of behavior? Lester offered two questions that influenced his evaluations of books: "Does [the book] accurately represent the black perspective?" and "Will it be relevant to black children?" Of course these questions are key, but Lester failed (or perhaps refused) to characterize those aspects of black perspective and relevance that white writers were unlikely to know about, or if they knew, would be loathe to reveal.

The opportunity to clarify his point was in Lester's own observation of the differences of critical reception of two of his works, *To Be a*

Slave (1968) and *Black Folktales* (1969). Lester explains:

> *The latter… has not been reviewed nearly as extensively and will definitely not be getting any prizes. And the reason to me is clear. The latter is directed totally toward black children…. [To Be a Slave] is more easily accessible to whites than the other. Whites have to open themselves a little more to dig Black Folktales… they have to meet me on my ground.*[11]

To Be a Slave, a Newbery Honor Book, was a collection of excerpts from the testimonials of former slaves, gathered as a part of the work of the Federal Writers Project in the 1930s, and the slave narratives written or narrated by escaped slaves, up to the Civil War. *To Be a Slave* is a powerful and necessary introduction to a body of American literature of which most young people, black and white, remain completely unaware. The voices of the slaves, however, inspire pathos, whether they describe outrageous cruelty by whites—

> *They whipped my father 'cause he looked at a slave they killed and cried.*
> **Roberta Manson, Library of Congress** [12]

—or individual acts of resistance by fellow slaves—

> *One day I saw the foreman slap a nigger for drinking at the dipper too long. The nigger picked up a shovel and slam him in the head and run.*

Lest this incident appear to describe a triumphant assertion of power, the speaker inserts a contextualizing explanation, insisting upon the victim status of the rebellious 'nigger:'

> *Back in the slavery days they didn't do something and run. They run before they did it, 'cause they knew that if they struck a white man, there wasn't going to be a nigger. In them days, they run to keep from doing something.* **Anonymous, Library of Congress** [13]

Focus on the black man's act of resistance is lessened; his ultimate powerlessness is brought to the foreground.

Black Folktales also introduces an important body of literature. However, these stories are, as Lester tells Woods, "directed totally toward" a black audience. Also, they do not ameliorate acts of resistive violence, but celebrate them. *Black Folktales* includes "High John the Conqueror" and "Stagolee," stories characterized by their sexual and violent content. Lester narrates the trickster John tales and the "badman" exploits of Stagolee in the voice of a 1960s militant. The effect is a startling unveiling of the voice of resistance that had always existed in the voice of the slave. In "High John the Conqueror," we receive a description of plantation life in Mississippi:

John lived on this plantation in Mississippi.... They had plantations so bad up in there, and the white folks was so mean, that the rattlesnakes wouldn't even bite 'em. Fraid they'd poison themselves. Snakes only bit niggers. White folks was so mean up there, they'd shoot a nigger just to bet on whether the body would fall frontwards or backwards. And then they'd go whup the dead nigger's mama if the body fell the wrong way.[14]

What Lester did not explain to Woods was that the national mythology as understood by the slaves was often a tale of violence and mayhem. He did not say that much of black resistance to slavery and the extended oppressions of Jim Crow, prior to Emancipation and the Civil Rights Movement, had been verbal, comprising forms of expressiveness that, had whites been fully aware, would have been squelched like their African languages. That these verbal resistances existed to prepare black adults, and the children who listened, to fight and circumvent the inequalities of the world shaped by slavery in ways that were just as deliberate and purposeful as the ways that white children were taught, through their parents' stories, to expect their white privilege. Lester did not explain what Woods should have known: that the literary products of black people would reflect the worldview, knowledge, and codes of the oppressed. That those worldviews challenged the views that whites held of black people, and of themselves. Ironically, black people had faith in white America. What else could explain this country's survival?

Instead, in a second letter, Lester says:

White writers are so dishonest. Seldom have they written what they could have and should have, which is, the white side of racism. I'd like to see a children's novel about a little white boy who goes with his father to a lynching.... White writers think they can write sympathetic, cloying little books about blacks. Who needs white pity?.... Where are the books for children that deal with whites and their racism? They don't exist, because it is easier to be paternalistic than honest. [15]

With this installment, the friendly correspondence apparently came to a close.

The conversation between Woods and Lester illustrates the different goals and perspectives of white and black intellectuals in the good books debate, each concerned more with his own color-coded population. Woods's idea that "black books" were for white people contended with Lester's idea that "black books" were for blacks first, and perhaps for those whites who were willing to come halfway across the racial divide. Works like William Armstrong's *Sounder* (1969), or Theodore Taylor's *The Cay* (1969) were probably among those that Woods considered to be the best of the books about blacks. These books were well-structured novels and quite readable; however, they did not satisfy Lester's "good books" criteria: Does the book accurately represent the black perspective? Will it be relevant to black children?

These works and others like them can be described briefly:

1. Black characters tended to be vaguely drawn, ill-conceived, or, like Mark Twain's Jim, motivated by the writer's goals more than by their own "fictional reality." Or, like Harriet Beecher Stowe's Uncle Tom, these characters were long-suffering and silent, evoking tears and pity, rarely revealing attitudes of anger, resistance, self-preservation, or any flicker of self-consciousness.

2. In social problem novels, social structures were rarely critiqued, but tended to be presented as absolute qualities of life. The causes of black suffering and realistic avenues for relief were rarely examined in the novel's conflict.

3. Story conflict and resolution tended to be located with the white characters. Black protagonists were passive respondents.

4. Historical fictions tended to be thinly veiled apologia for white oppression, using black characters as mouthpieces. Some works featuring black images were not about black people at all, but used blacks as background materials to lend poignancy to the troubled white characters.

With the emergence of a core of black writers, there began to exist a few alternative examples of what a "good black book" might be. Black writers applied the accepted standards of good fiction to their black fictional characters:

1. Black protagonists are active, not passive; fully developed, not flat. Active characters move towards change and are consistently motivated in their actions and perceptions;

2. Social structures are critiqued rather than being uncritically presented as unassailable reality;

3. Stories are complex, involving internal and external conflict;

4. Solutions to problems are devised and carried out by the active black characters, not by *deux ex machina* white characters who appear in the nick of time for the rescue;

5. Black characters are interesting, complex, flawed moral beings.

Black artists demonstrated that the same artistic criteria that, presumably, governed the evaluation of "white" books would have to be adhered to in the creation and evaluation of books offered as multicultural materials for children. For art's sake, writers would have to relearn a basic lesson in story writing: point of view.

Point of view may be the single most important aspect in the creation of story. In the children's book category of the art wars, this matter of point of view was, in fact, the most difficult. How could white writers, complacent with the social, historical and economic hegemony of a white America, truthfully represent a "black" point of view without condemning themselves, and white people generally, in the pages of children's books?   The failure of white artists to overcome their tendency to exonerate themselves and America by violating black fictional point of view led black artists and critics to conclude that the condition of their whiteness would prevent white artists from writing with integrity about black people in America.

Naturally, the white establishment and its artists rejected this conclusion. However, the provocation of this assertion might have had more to do with prodding the advancement of crosscultural book art for children than any other single feature of this discourse. White artists had to "come humble," admit that valuable lessons awaited them if they would enter into this black space wearing the robe of the suppliant; they would have to renounce the minstrel model of black representation, "prove" their capacity to sing the blues of black cultural story. And ultimately, they would have to step up to the stage and hold their own in the jam session of their American story lives. Equally important, the art wars led to a vigorous questioning of the notion of "the black experience," and to the question "What is black art?" These developments were instructive for artists, black and white.

> My work requires me to think about how free I can be as an African-American woman writer in my genderized, sexualized, wholly racialized world. To think about (and wrestle with) the full implications of my situation leads me to consider what happens when other writers work in a highly and historically racialized society. For them, as for me, imagining is not merely looking or looking at; nor is it taking oneself intact into the other. It is, for the purposes of the work, becoming. [16]

In the passage above, Morrison states the problem of the artist succinctly, not apart from the politics of meaning, but through it. "Becoming," after all, is the challenge of living. It is also the challenge of the writer for the reader: can the writer inhabit a world so completely and render her discoveries so skillfully that the reader loses a part of herself to become a part of that other world? The writer cannot take herself, intact, into the "other." She must lose parts of herself to become the "other." How much self can the writer stand to give up in order to gain the story of the other? (How much of our own selves are we able to know in our wholly racialized, genderized, sexualized world?) How much does the writer (and the reader) benefit from that loss? I believe these are the questions of the fully engaged artist. Writing is a process of losing and gaining the self.

In a historical context where white means power, and black means powerlessness (or less-ness), this process of the 'white' losing in order to become 'black' is a frightening prospect. It's no wonder it happens so infrequently. Still, the writings of white artists are permeated with black presence, though the writers may permit the black body only a "shadowless participation in the dominant cultural body."[17] Toni Morrison has revisited the canon literature in search of a shadow:

> *Explicit or implicit, the Africanist presence informs in compelling and inescapable ways the texture of American literature. It is a dark and abiding presence, there for the literary imagination as both a visible and an invisible mediating force. Even, and especially, when American texts are not "about" Africanist presences or characters or narrative or idiom, the shadow hovers in implication, in sign, in line of demarcation."[18]*

If Morrison is right—that blackness is present even in the absences resulting from mannerly silences on matters of race, gender, and sex—our readings of books for American youth become much richer; bridges appear between worlds that were reputedly disparate and unrelated.

A good example comes in the work of Margaret Wise Brown. Brown's work, generally, is notable for its unobtrusiveness, its politeness. She is certainly not viewed as an artist who had anything to say on the subject of race. Yet at least two books exist outside of her usual production criteria.

Night and Day (1942), and *Black and White* (1944), are full of the shadows of black presence. Produced during the years of severe racial strife, when African Americans were being Jim Crowed in America and six million Jews were being exterminated abroad, these two works offer a utopian wish camouflaged, thinly, by anthropomorphism and fantasy. *Night and Day* discusses color differences, and the opposing attributes assigned to those colors, through a story about two cats (literally), one black and one white. The white cat is afraid of the dark. She is not afraid of the stars, the wind, and the moon, but of "Things That Never Were." "'What are Things That Never Were?' asked the black cat. 'Ghosts and goblins,' purred the white cat behind closed eyes."[19] When the white cat opens her eyes to realize that her fears of blackness (or night) are based on nothing tangible, she follows the black cat into the night when "The world is quiet.... [and] all our own."

Black and White is more daring. This picture book posits a world composed of only one color: black.

> *Once there was a story in which everything was black.*
> *Black as ink.*
> *Black as the night.*
> *Black.*
> *This was the story about a black man who lived in the*
> *black country of Wales in a big black house and ate*
> *black bean soup and blackberries every day for his lunch.* [20]

The "black man" is not a "Negro," but a man whose features and attire suggest the Caucasian. The black man's blackness seems to be entirely superficial and voluntary. Everything in his tiny personal world is black. Even his dreams feature images of a sheep, a bear, and an angel, all black. Then one night his dreams are invaded by a mysterious speck of white that grows into a snowman, "only the snowman was really a lady, so she married the black man," and they live happily ever after, mixing black things together with white things.

Night and Day and *Black and White*, like Brown's better known works, *Goodnight Moon* and *Runaway Bunny*, are about overcoming fear. The picture book images are designed to reassure rather than disturb or excite. In *Night and Day*, a child's fear of the dark is represented as harmless kittens, images reassuring to any child. In *Black and White*, the black man is really "white," standing in an inescapable and mysteriously cast shadow. The accompanying texts provide deconstructions of ethnocentrism and racism in baby talk.

In *Black and White*, Brown steps from behind the puppet show of animals and allows a direct association between picture book and real life by creating a "black man" and "white lady," two adult figures. Ironically, she must depend upon the foregrounding of color (and the background reference to Wales) to hinder the natural association between the term, "black man," and men of African origin.

What is painful and funny about *Black and White* is the terrible tension within the images: a black man who is not a black man; a white "lady" who, by American definitions, is not a lady anymore once she marries this "black man"! But Brown cannot shackle story meaning, just as white America could not deny humanity to black people by edict. The truth of the story defies the "white" lie of euphemistic imaging. The writhings in these books remind us that the painful effort to contain meaning has always been a necessary part of racial dominance. Of course, one can't be sure whether the contortions were Brown's, her illustrator's, or her editor's. What seems clear is Brown's impulse to comment on black presence, racial harmony, and the naturalness of diversity in a book for mainstream distribution. What is also made visually clear by Brown's efforts is the tradition of obscuring the black image, especially when the subject is explicitly racial.

It seems Brown's readers were at least suspicious of her content. One admirer of Brown's work[21] later answered the charges by denying any shadow of black presence in these works, as though he were defending her virtue. The single major biography on Brown's life and work does not discuss the artist's conception of these two works,[22] so we are left with the works themselves.

The tradition of racial obscurantism continues, especially in works for children that embed a serious critique of fundamental American principles and the structures of racial supremacy. Motivated by fear of the racial subject, and fear of too much truth, obscurantist artists create art that is deeply flawed. However, by removing fear from the artist's palette, I discovered the sideways truth of irony. If Brown's "black man" is not an obscured African, what is the blackness that he wears?

— — —

...my job is to transmit to you all the memories I have within me. Memories of the past.[23]

In *The Giver* (1993), Lois Lowry posits a world free of memory, free of the past. In fact, all areas of conflict have been removed. All uncertainty has been eliminated because all choice has been rendered unnecessary. There is peace and harmony, total employment. There is no overpopulation, no hunger. Death is managed. Natural sexual impulses are suppressed through drugs; childbearing is a low-status job assigned to girls who show no potential for anything else; all jobs are assigned. Violence is unknown. A perfect, uncomplicated world where sameness is valued over everything.

The protagonist, Jonas, is happy as far as he knows, until he is assigned the prestigious job of The Receiver, until he meets The Giver and begins his life work. He must receive and remember all of the memories of the past that his community has forgotten. Jonas, through his training, begins to know what it is to feel life and pain.

The Giver can be read as utopian futurist fantasy that serves as an allegory. The "future" of Lowry's Community is here. We are the people who desire to obliterate memory of the past, because it is too painful. We are the people who use language ritualistically, depriving words and expressions of real meaning. We are the people who drug ourselves into numbness. We are the people creating the law and science of surrogate parenthood. We are the people who will drive nature into extinction. We are the society that segregates on the basis of color while advocating "colorblindness" as a virtue. *The Giver* is all of modern America's wishes come true.

The Africans are gone. We meet Lily, Rosemary, Asher, Caleb, Katherine, Gabriel, Yoshiko, Andrei, Fiona, Benjamin, Larissa, Edna, Pierre, Inger, Isaac, Madeline. The names are cultural remnants of Western civilizations. None conjure the East (except the mysterious Yoshiko), Middle East, or Africa. Yet the shadow of an African presence is everywhere in the novel's conflict, disturbing the peacefulness of the novel because it is being thrown by a figure that is noticeably not in the picture.

Jonas runs away from his "perfect" Community and, as the novel closes, he approaches another place. From a distance he can see their red, blue, and yellow lights; he can hear music and singing. (Who could these people be?!) With perfection behind him, he runs toward a place that seems to promise the discord and harmonies of love, longing, struggle, anger, stupidity, brilliance, joy, pain, and remembering. A paradise of imperfection and human striving. But one wonders what Jonas will do in this unseen paradise, this place that seems to represent the opposite of the "perfect" Community.

Is Lowry guilty of using a "savage" unknown as a "denotative and connotative blackness that African peoples have come to signify,..."[24] in the black/white trope common to American literature and life? a fictional, romanticized, black space of possibility? The novel's structure seems to invite this reading. The image of Jonas running towards the romanticized unknown evokes the image of the first arrivals of the European to Africa and the pre-Christian Americas, men looking to escape the restrictive structures of one place, running toward the promise of freedom and lack of restraint in another. As if realizing this unfortunate potential, Lowry closes:

> Behind [Jonas], across vast distances of space and time, from the place he had left, he thought he heard music too. But perhaps it was only an echo. [25]

Let's hope not. If the Community has found its own music—its own life—then the repeat of an unfortunate political and literary history need not take place.

In *The Giver* colors suggest vibrancy and the uncertainties of life, and they are the promise at the end of the novel. In *Toning the Sweep* (1993), by Angela Johnson, color is the first reality, the first memory.

Toning the Sweep is about a physically present African American family; however, Johnson also employs a color-deficit model in her story-imaging. The family is culturally identifiable through geography, story, voice, and tradition—not by the writer's descriptions of skin color. The novel, however, is full of color—the colors of the natural world, the colors of healing.

> *My grandmama Ola says that yellow is the first color she ever remembers seeing...Her mama dressed her in yellow.... Their house sat between two willows. They were yellow in spring.*[26]

Yellow permeates the novel. It is a color of conflicting meanings. We discover that the grandmother, Ola, is dying of cancer. Yellow has long been considered the sign of sickness. But it is also the color of money, gold, a symbol of affluence—another kind of sickness. Significantly, it was a new Buick with a white interior that precipitated Ola's husband's murder back in Alabama in 1964—some white men thought he ought not to be able to afford it, and killed him. His murder sent Ola running to the desert to find some space, some colors other than the blacks and whites of Alabama. Still, and perhaps most powerfully in the novel, yellow is also the sign of the sun, which is life. The sun often signifies fire. The desert is a place of fire and stories of water.

Toning the Sweep is full of ambiguities. Nothing is just one thing, but many. No story or perception is absolute; things shift and change in time, and in the changing light. The "blackness" of this black family both is and is not significant. Emily's friend, David, both is and is not American Indian. He is an orphan who chooses to retrieve a story that makes him more peaceful with himself.

To achieve the complexity of point of view relevant to her story, Johnson builds a foundation of complex story that relinquishes, when needed, the stories of the African, the Native American, the African American, and others. The novel's diversity is structured—not applied like a veneer, or plugged in like a finger in a leaky dike. It is in David Two Star's individual account of The Emergence; in Emily's story of resistance and self-assertion; in Ola's story of escape out of Alabama, and her discovery of "another planet out here" in the desert; in the stories of the laughing Aunts. The stories of the people exist as a diversity and a spiritual healing power.

In *Toning the Sweep* black people are real manifestations of history, but their skin color is not emphasized as a descriptive. The stories that the people carry describe them. The story of skin color is a narrow story of two colors: black and white. It is a story of murder. For Angela Johnson, it is a story of the past that needs to be "toned."

Toning the Sweep takes its title from Emily's recovery of an old southern ritual, "ringing the dead to heaven." It is Emily who "start[s] thinking about restless souls and ancestors" and decides to perform the ritual before they leave Ola's desert refuge to return to Ohio. Instead of a sweep, Emily and her mother will tone the dead to rest by striking the water tower.

> The water tower was as important in the desert as the sweep used to be in Alabama. Granddaddy would understand…. The hammer shines in the bright sun; then we strike metal. Again and again, until the sound seems natural, a part of the wind.[27]

As Emily tones the water tower, Angela Johnson seems to be asking, can we ring this story of two colors to rest? The novel gives us a story, and a ritual, of healing.

— — —

Fear breeds a desire to escape. To avoid. To lie. To create distances. Both of these novels include stories of escape as a response to fear and moral fatigue. And both stories confirm the impossibility of escape. We cannot escape from ourselves.

The Giver works as allegory—to reveal a situation, make it visible. *Toning the Sweep* is more intimate, asking a much more personal question: How will you live with your past?

— — —

In this fictitious evolution of a story art, I might be tempted to draw a line from the tradition of avoidance techniques and silences of white privilege characterized here in the works of Margaret Wise Brown, to the shadows of black presence in this novel by Lois Lowry, making her a literary daughter. But I won't. It would not be true, or not true enough anyway. Lowry's novel makes no excuses. The absence of African presence from her story suggests, rather than the usual racial arrogance or political timidity, a deliberate intention to direct her allegorical light to the culture of technology, control, and destruction over which third world nations and colonized peoples have little control.

Lois Lowry's story is for the children of privilege first, though not exclusively. The absence of The Black can be read ironically, and instructively. In *The Giver*, what is absent is always potentially and dangerously present.

I am tempted, as well, to draw a line from the liberation narratives of the escaped African to Angela Johnson. And I will. The men and women who were able to escape from a mental slavery wrote their stories, for abolition and for posterity. African Americans have often betrayed the bold example of their storytelling by creating a simplicity of silence (or a simplicity of black and white) that has left our youth without sufficient information or storied complexity to make clear judgements about themselves and others.

Angela Johnson's story is for black readers first, though not exclusively. She is specifically addressing the silences constructed and maintained within the black community. (It is not just white people who create debilitating silences.) Johnson speaks through them, and against them. Emily must be told the tales that might make it possible for her to live with the past and choose a different future.

Considered together, these two novels can contribute to a short-list tradition of "true" art in racial representation in the young adult novel, taking on the complexity of our "colored" lives and calling for the imaginative participation of the reader in creating new codes of behavior and a more epic myth of nation.

Within these fictional worlds exists the possibility of "becoming." This is young adult literature, if it encourages a discursive exchange within and between our communities, that might improve our lives and not debase it.

Notes

1.   John Gardner, *On Moral Fiction*. New York: Basic Books, 1978, p.9.

2.   Ibid., p.5.

3.   Ibid., p.5.

4.   Toni Morrison, *Playing in the Dark: Whiteness and the Literary Imagination*. Cambridge, MA: Harvard University Press, 1992. p.9-10.

5.   Ibid., p.9.

6.   Dianne Johnson, *Telling Tales: The Pedagogy and Promise of African American Literature for Youth*. Westport, CT: Greenwood Press, 1990. p.12.

7.   Jan, *On Children's Literature*, 39, (qtd. in Johnson, p.7).

8.   Johnson, p.7.

9.   Julius Lester and George Woods, "Black and White: An Exchange," reprinted in *The Black American in Books for Children: Readings in Racism*, eds. Donnarae MacCann and Gloria Woodard. Meutchen, NJ: Scarecrow Press, 1985. p.66.

10.   Ibid., p.67.

11.   Ibid., p.68.

12.   Julius Lester, *To Be a Slave*. New York: Scholastic, 1968. p.33.

13.   Ibid., p.29.

14.   Julius Lester, *Black Folktales*. New York: Grove Press, 1969. p.94.

15.   Lester, *The Black American*, p.72.

16.   Morrison, p.4.

17. Ibid., p.10.

18. Ibid., p.46-7.

19. Margaret Wise Brown, *Night and Day*. New York: Harper, 1942.

20. Margaret Wise Brown, *Black and White*. New York: Harper, 1944.

21. Eugene M. Scheel, *Margaret Wise Brown, The Foremost Innovator of Contemporary Literature for Children*. George Washington University, 1969. Unpublished Dissertation. Scheel writes: "...a small but vocal segment of the buying public tendered some erroneous interpretations to the purpose behind the books. Margaret did not specifically have the Black or Caucasian Race in mind; she was only interested in projecting an atmosphere of contrasting periods of time and philosophies of life" p.137.

22. Leonard S. Marcus, *Margaret Wise Brown: Awakened by the Moon*. Boston, MA: Beacon Press, 1992.

23. Lois Lowry, *The Giver*. New York: Bantam, 1993. p.77.

24. Morrison, p.6.

25. Lowry, p.180.

26. Angela Johnson, *Toning the Sweep*. New York: Orchard, 1993. p.1.

27. Ibid., p.99.

Additional Works Cited

Armstrong, William. *Sounder*. New York: Harper, 1969.

———. *Goodnight Moon*. New York: Harper, 1947.

———. *The Runaway Bunny*. New York: Harper, 1942.

Hamilton, Virginia. *M.C. Higgins, the Great*. New York: Macmillan, 1974.

———. *The Planet of Junior Brown*. New York: Macmillan, 1974.

Taylor, Mildred D. *Roll of Thunder, Hear My Cry*. New York: Dial, 1975.

Taylor, Theodore. *The Cay*. New York: Doubleday, 1969.

ABOUT THE AUTHOR

Opal Moore writes poetry and fiction. Her work has appeared in *Callaloo* magazine, *The African American Review,* and *Ancestral House: The Black Short Story in the Americas and Europe,* an anthology. She is co-editor of "Cultural Pluralism" for the *Children's Literature Association Quarterly* and is Associate Professor of English at Hollins College in Virginia.

This essay is based on a workshop presented at the Virginia Hamilton Conference on April 21, 1995.

One Smiling Grandma by Ann Marie Linden, pictures by Lynne Russell.

13

ALL IN MY FAMILY
PICTURE BOOKS REFLECTING FAMILIES' CULTURAL DIVERSITY
SUE MCCLEAF NESPECA

THERE HAS BEEN much emphasis in recent years on the importance of the family unit in a child's life. Even our government has stressed the importance of family life and ways the family can be involved in improving the quality of a child's life. Parental involvement in a child's education is cited as the major reason for a child's success in school, and the involvement of the entire family in the emerging literacy skills of young children has proven effective.

Family structures have changed over the years. Families can be headed by aunts, uncles, grandparents, guardians, or foster parents. Families can be single-parent households, extended families, "blended" families, interracial families, or homes with two adults of the same sex raising a child. Each family is unique, and members may be from different ethnic backgrounds. It is important that all children feel pride in their own ethnic and racial heritage. What better way is there for children to take pride in their roots than by having family members share their background, their family histories, and family stories.

There are many picture books that can help children relate to their own family history or the family histories of their peers. However, this cultural understanding can be greatly increased by sharing picture books reflecting families' cultural diversities. Through the illustrations, an understanding of the different types of families represented in our country or other countries can be greatly enhanced. By using multicultural picture books, children can gain an awareness of and appreciation for the diversity of other families and can develop respect for their peers.

BOOKS CELEBRATING FAMILY HISTORIES OR DISCOVERING ANCESTRY

Every child in the world is special by having his/her own unique family history. By exploring ancestry and by having family members share cherished memories, children can experience a sense of pride and belonging. They can be encouraged to write and illustrate one of their own family stories after reading (or having adults share) picture books that explore family histories or ancestries. Following are several picture books that do this successfully. The illustrations in the books convey all the different kinds of families in the world, explore families' special relationships, or recall memorable experiences of growing up.

In Angela Johnson's *Tell Me a Story, Mama*, a young girl asks her mother questions at bedtime, so that her mother can share stories about the special moments in their family's life. David Soman uses expressive watercolors to display the rich emotions a mother and daughter share during this important bedtime ritual.

Of course, all families are different, and children soon realize that these differences can sometimes create barriers between them and their peers. In *Families Are Different*, Nico realizes that she and her sister, Angel, are unlike other children in her class, having been born in Korea and now adopted by an American family. She soon realizes, however, that other classmates also have varying family backgrounds. Author/illustrator Nina Pellegrini's illustrations depict the different kinds of families there are in the world: biracial families, households with single parents, children of divorced parents, children who live with grandparents, children with stepparents or half-brothers or sisters, and parents with adopted children.

In Mary Hoffman's *Boundless Grace*, Grace, who lives in America, is united with her father, whom she barely remembers, when visiting his new African home. He has since remarried and has more children. Though getting to meet her new stepmother, half-brother and half-sister is difficult for Grace, she soon realizes that Nana is right—"Families are what you make them." Vivid watercolor drawings by Caroline Binch portray this very different life in Africa—from clothing to food, to animals such as crocodiles, and colorful market scenes. To make her illustrations totally authentic, Binch made two trips to Gambia, photographing backgrounds and people for the story.

Some authors successfully share their own family history through picture books. Allen Say has illustrated several picture books about his ancestry, with *Grandfather's Journey* winning the 1994 Caldecott Medal for its illustrations. His striking paintings elucidate the conflict he feels between his love for America and his love for Japan and how he would like to be in both places at the same time. He realizes how similar he is to his grandfather, who had the same feelings about the two countries, and who related his cross-cultural experiences to his grandson. These same cross-cultural experiences are recounted in Say's *Tree of Cranes*. In that book a Japanese mother, who lived in California when she was young, decides to share her childhood remembrances of the tradition of Christmas with her Japanese son, who has never heard of the religious holiday. She decorates a tree with candles and origami cranes and gives him a kite for a present. Traditional Japanese customs are depicted in the radiant watercolor illustrations.

Sherley Anne Williams recalls her childhood experiences of picking cotton in Fresno in the picture book *Working Cotton*. The book won a Caldecott Honor and a Coretta Scott King Award for illustration. The hazy sky in the early hours of morning and the migrant family's life of toil and sweat are dramatically brought to life through acrylic paintings by artist Carole Byard.

Donald Crews, also a Caldecott Honor Book winner, relates what it was like visiting his grandma in the summertime in Florida in the book *Bigmama's*. Friends and family were there to share stories and have fun with during the long, hot months. His other book of family history is *Short Cut*, a story in which he and other children take a short cut home by walking on train tracks, barely escaping an approaching train. In both books he uses watercolors, gouache paints, and intriguing graphic design to share childhood memories. Particularly interesting are the graphics in *Short Cut*, with the increasing size of the letters for the sound "Whoo" as the train gets closer and closer to the children and the endpapers of the book, where the words "Klak, Klak, Klakity Klak" are repeatedly written, reminiscent of train tracks.

INTERGENERATIONAL STORIES

Children are truly fortunate when they have grandparents, aunts, or uncles willing to recount family memories or family history. Not only can this sharing time be cherished, but children have an opportunity to bond with older relatives and to gain an understanding of family history and how one fits into that family, which can build self-esteem. (Note artist Lynne Russell's illustration of a young girl and her smiling grandmother pictured at the beginning of this chapter.) There are numerous picture books that explore these intergenerational family bonds, and several will be mentioned here.

Most intergenerational picture books center on the relationship between a child and his/her grandmother or grandfather. In Arthur Dorros's two books *Abuela* and *Isla*, Rosalba and her grandmother soar through the sky (in Rosalba's imagination) exploring family history. In *Abuela*, Rosalba's grandmother narrates sights she saw in Manhattan when she first came to America. In *Isla*, they travel to the island where Abuela grew up, and Rosalba meets relatives and hears family stories. Elisa Kleven, illustrator of both books, uses a mixed-media collage of watercolors, pastels, ink, and cut paper in a folklore motif to give these flights of fancy special child appeal.

Several books have been written with the theme of a quilt being made by family members. Georgia Guback uses bright colors reminiscent of the Hawaiian island setting for her book *Luka's Quilt*. The intricate cut-paper collage is particularly appropriate for the quilt designs displayed. The traditional Hawaiian quilt that Tutu makes as a gift for her granddaughter Luka is not what Luka had hoped for, and the girl's disappointment causes a strain in their relationship until Tutu finds a compromise.

A quilt is also central to the story *The Patchwork Quilt* written by Valerie Flournoy. Grandma begins making a quilt from scraps of material left from family members' clothing in order to tell the story of the family's life. When she becomes ill, Tanya and her mom finish it, to fulfill the family tradition. *Patchwork Quilt* gained the Coretta Scott King Award for illustration for illustrator Jerry Pinkney. In the sequel, *Tanya's Reunion*, Tanya goes with her grandmother to Virginia, where Grandma grew up, to help prepare for a family reunion. While there, Grandma shares family memories with her granddaughter through the history of the farm. Pinkney illustrates both books in muted watercolors and pencil. He is especially successful in showing the love between grandmother and granddaughter when they return to the family homestead.

The particularly close bond between a grandparent and grandchild is explored in numerous picture books. Three mentioned here have especially striking, vibrant art. Ann Marie Linden's *One Smiling Grandma* is a counting book that shares the sights and sounds of the Caribbean through the adventures of a young girl and her grandmother. Illustrator Lynne Russell, a talented painter and printmaker, uses bright watercolors to make this tropical island setting especially inviting. David Soman's touching watercolor pictures accompany a poignant story by Angela Johnson entitled *When I Am Old With You*. A young grandchild imagines what it would be like to be as old as her grandfather and to enjoy many of his daily activities such as playing cards or walking along the ocean. And Pat Cummings's dark, foreboding pictures shadow a young boy's fear of thunderstorms in Mary Stolz's *Storm in the Night*. The boy is comforted only when his grandfather explains that he also feared thunderstorms when he was young.

Several intergenerational stories with grandparent/grandchild themes take place in other countries. Ted Lewin effectively uses black-and-white illustrations to represent the past and watercolor illustrations to portray the present in *The Always Prayer Shawl,* written by Sheldon Oberman. In that book, Adam, a young Jewish boy in Czarist Russia, and his family leave the country for a new home. His grandfather, following Jewish tradition, hands down his prayer shawl to his grandson, as Adam himself will do one day. The powerful image of the shawl is even reflected in the endpapers of the book.

Ann Grifalconi is author and illustrator of two titles about Osa and her grandmother, who live in Africa. In *The Village of Round and Square Houses,* (a Caldecott Honor Book), Osa's grandmother tells her why the men in their village live in square houses and the women live separately in round ones. In *Osa's Pride,* Grandma warns Osa about having too much pride by sharing a story about pride that is depicted in the colorful story cloth she is making. Particularly striking are Grifalconi's illustrations of the bright story cloth showing an African woman carrying eggs in a basket on her head. The basket is full of eggs, but, being vain and holding her head high, the woman does not realize the eggs are falling out. In *Sitti's Secrets,* by Naomi Shihab Nye, children are transported through Nancy Carpenter's illustrations to a Palestinian village on the West Bank, where Mona visits her grandmother (Sitti). Family traditions are shared, and Mona decides to write to the President of the United States, asking for peace in relations between her country and her grandmother's part of the world.

Intergenerational stories can also center on other family members. In two books written by his wife, Gloria Pinkney, Jerry Pinkney again executes his magic in warmly colored, sunlit-kissed, full-page illustrations. *Back Home* finds eight-year-old Ernestine leaving her family's home up North to visit Uncle June, Aunt Beula, and Cousin Jack in Lumberton, North Carolina, where she was born and where her Mama grew up. In the sequel, *Sunday Outing,* she rides the trolley with her Great Aunt Odessa to the train station, while hearing family stories about her Great Uncle Ariah, the trainman.

In Margaree King Mitchell's, *Uncle Jed's Barbershop,* illustrator James Ransome uses full-spread dramatic oil paintings to help tell a touching story. Sarah Jean's Uncle Jed, the only black barber in the county, finally realizes his dream of saving enough money to open his barbershop. Particularly touching is Ransome's illustration of Uncle Jed running the clippers on the back of Sarah Jean's neck while she is holding a doll and the family dog is watching.

Paintings done in watercolors, pastels, and colored pencils by author/illustrator Ann Grifalconi accompany the story of Sissy, who is feeling *Kinda Blue* one day because it seems her whole family has no time for her, and she is missing her Pa, who died when she was a baby girl. In one moving scene, Uncle Dan makes her pick an ear of corn filled with red and blue kernels, showing her that all ears of corn are different. This ear needs the same love and care that other ears of corn do though. In a double-page, close-up illustration, Uncle Dan hugs the crying girl, saying that even though she misses her father, the rest of the family all love and care for her.

An aunt is the central character in Elizabeth Howard's *Aunt Flossie's Hats (and Crab Cakes Later)*. Sarah and Susan's favorite day of the week is Sunday when they go visit their Great-Great-Aunt Flossie. After rummaging through mounds of hat boxes, they pick out a hat and hear a story from Aunt Flossie's past that revolves around the hat. James Ransome uses thick brush strokes of oil paint in his pictures showing the girls examining the hats, wearing the hats, and going to a restaurant later with Aunt Flossie to devour crab cakes.

Of course, intergenerational stories can also revolve around older friends or acquaintances of the story's main characters, rather than their relatives. Examples are three books by the famous storyteller and artist Patricia Polacco. In *Chicken Sunday*, a young girl teaches Stewart and Winston, her two male friends, how to decorate eggs the way her bubbie from the old country taught her. The three intend to sell the eggs to buy Stewart and Winston's gramma, Miss Eula, a treasured hat, because Miss Eula is so special to all of them. In *Mrs. Katz and Tush*, African American Larnel becomes friends with his neighbor, Mrs. Katz, through an abandoned kitten. Mrs. Katz shares stories of her Jewish heritage, which Larnel relates to his black history. The two celebrate a Passover seder together. In Polacco's story, *Pink and Say*, Say Curtis describes meeting black soldier Pinkus Aylee during the Civil War when Say is wounded and left for dead. Pinkus, lost from his company, takes Say home with him to help the boy recover. Pinkus's mother attempts to hide her son and Say, but she is killed. Both boys are later captured by Confederate troops, but Say survives Andersonville Prison, while Pinkus is immediately killed. In all three books, Polacco sets the scene, by juxtaposing her ethnically diverse characters and moving images against stark white backgrounds. It is her little touches, such as folk art or real photographs of her family members mixed in with her drawings, that make her books so appealing and distinctive.

FAMILY LIFE FOR CHILDREN GROWING UP IN AMERICA WITH DUAL CULTURES

Many children growing up in America today are originally from other countries, and even though their family may embrace American culture, they also want to preserve the culture from their homeland. Native American children, too, grow up in dual cultures. Most of the books written about these children with dual cultures use photographs for illustrations. Authors George Ancona, Tricia Brown, and Diane Hoyt-Goldsmith have produced several titles. In *Powwow* photojournalist Ancona allows the reader to view the largest powwow held in the United States. In *Earth Daughter*, he shows Alicia, a member of the Acoma Pueblo, learning the art of pottery-making from her family. In *Hello, Amigos!* Tricia Brown presents a Mexican American child's special birthday traditions. In *Lee Ann*, she shows how a Vietnamese refugee family celebrates Tet, the Vietnamese New Year. *Cherokee Summer*, by Hoyt-Goldsmith presents such Cherokee traditions as the hog fry, the stomp dance, and basket-weaving. Her book *Hoang Anh* describes a young Vietnamese American boy's life.

Some other titles using photographic essays to show children living in dual cultures include: Ginger Gordon's *My Two Worlds,* about a young girl who lives in New York but still has ties to her family's homeland in Puerto Plata; Joan Hewett's *Hector Lives in the United States Now,* about a ten-year-old born in Guadalajara, Mexico, and now living in Los Angeles; Marcia Keegan's *Pueblo Boy: Growing Up in Two Worlds,* showing a ten-year-old's daily life in New Mexico; Russ Kendall's *Eskimo Boy* about life in an Inupiaq Eskimo village; *Lion Dancer,* by Kate Waters and Madeline Slovenz-Low, in which six-year-old Ernie Wan participates for the first time in a Lion Dance for Chinese New Year; and Susan Kuklin's *How My Family Lives in America,* describing the life of African American Sanu, Hispanic American Eric, and Asian American April.

One of the few titles that does not use a photographic approach is Jane Resh Thomas's *Lights on the River*, illustrated with watercolors by Michael Dooling. This book tells the story of Teresa, daughter of hardworking Mexican American migrants, who remembers her grandmother and her Mexican customs from the past, such as the Christmas celebration of lighting candles along the river. Dooling's illustrations, reveal in a special way, the plight of the Hispanic migrant family.

FAMILY LIFE OF CHILDREN FROM AMERICA LIVING IN OTHER COUNTRIES

What do American children experience when they live in or visit other countries for an extended period of time? How do their families help them adjust to the differences they experience in their daily lives?

In *When Africa Was Home* Karen Lynn Williams relates the sentiments of one young boy, Peter, who was raised in Africa from infancy, and misses it dreadfully when his family moves back to America. When his father finds a job again in Africa, Peter is glad to move back to the only home he really remembers, and that he loves so much. Floyd Cooper elucidates these warm feelings by using bright and glowing colors, particularly the yellow, orange, and brown oil washes he uses so expressively. One can feel the warm brown earth that Peter experiences running barefoot in Africa and the icy cold snows he endures in America.

In *Masai and I* Virginia Kroll tells the story of Linda, an American girl studying the country of East Africa in school and imagining what her life would be like if she were a Masai, including going to her grandmother's 70th birthday party. Nancy Carpenter uses oil paints and pink colored-pencil lines to juxtapose, in double-page spreads, Linda's American life with that of the Masai life in her imagination,

When she was only eight-years-old, Nila Leigh wrote and illustrated *Learning to Swim in Swaziland: A Child's-Eye View of a Southern African Country.* Her parents took her there to live, and this book, in her own handwriting and with her own illustrations, documents some of her experiences. Nila wrote letters to her classmates in America, and it was from these letters that her story was born. She describes her school year, her friends, her daily life, food, a hut she lived in, and how she learned to swim. Her illustrations, simple crayon drawings, will appeal to children, who can relate to her child's-eye view of another country.

Vibrant watercolors are used by author and illustrator Caroline Binch in her book *Gregory Cool*, about a typical young American boy who spends four weeks visiting relatives in Tobago. Gregory wears sneakers and a backwards baseball cap and his favorite food is a hamburger. Arriving in Tobago, he finds he must live in a tiny house in excessive heat, and eat foods such as *bake* and *buljol*, sweet bread and coconut. Ms. Binch traveled to Tobago to research and paint *Gregory Cool*, and she captures the essence of this unique Caribbean island.

FAMILY LIFE FOR CHILDREN IN OTHER COUNTRIES

What is family life like for children in other countries? How are their lives similar to and different from life in America? By exploring other cultural traditions and different ways of life, children will learn to be more tolerant of others. They will also soon realize that children all over the world share many of the same feelings.

Some books explore basic differences. Edith Baer's books *This Is the Way We Eat Our Lunch* and *This Is the Way We Go to School* use rhymed texts to express differences in food and in the methods of transportation children use to get to school. Steve Bjorkman provides cheerful cartoon-like illustrations and a map in the back of both books so that readers can locate where the children described in the text live. *This Is My House,* written and illustrated by Arthur Dorros, shows children different types of housing around the world. Dorros also includes the words "This is my house" written in the thirteen different languages spoken by the people who live in the houses depicted.

Ken Heyman photographed differences in homes, food, methods of transportation and everyday activities in countries around the world for a series of books written by Ann Morris. Titles include *Bread, Bread, Bread; Hats, Hats, Hats; Loving; On the Go; Houses and Homes; Shoes; Tools;* and *Weddings.* Indexes include information on where the pictures were taken, along with a map to locate the countries. Through the engaging photos, children have a firsthand look at people and their lives in other countries of the world.

Other picture books share these similarities and differences in a more subtle manner. A few with especially engaging artwork are described here. Ted Lewin's luminous watercolor paintings accompany two books with Middle Eastern settings written by Florence Parry Heide and Judith Heide Gilliland. *The Day of Ahmed's Secret* describes a boy who has a special secret he wishes to share with his family, which must wait until after his day's work of hauling butane gas canisters for the family's business. His secret is that he has learned to write his name in Arabic. In *Sami and the Time of the Troubles,* a ten-year-old boy narrates his life with his Lebanese family. Part of his young life is spent above ground, and the rest underground in a basement shelter, to avoid being bombed. Lewin displays these contrasting times in the boy's life by a superb use of light and dark. While Sami is underground, dimly lit images appear on stark black backgrounds and the text is set in white ink. When Sami goes above ground, there is an infusion of light, with blue skies and scenes of bright flowers and peach orchards. The text is now printed in black, on light blue backgrounds. These illuminations and textual designs allow the reader to experience the emotions felt by the young boy who lives both above and below ground.

Author and illustrator Rachel Isadora made several trips to South Africa, where she witnessed scenes depicted in the bright watercolor illustrations of her two books *At the Crossroads* and *Over the Green Hills.* In the first title, Isadora describes how children living in the segregated townships of South Africa are separated from their fathers for months at a time while the fathers work in the mines. When it is time for the fathers to return, the children anxiously wait for them at the crossroads. In *Over the Green Hills,* Zolani, his mother, and young sister Noma journey many miles from their rural coastal home to visit his grandmother. Isadora's illustrations give an authentic glimpse of this area of South Africa. With mussels, dried fish, mielies, and a pumpkin, they make their way through fields, forests, farms, and over the green hills of the Transkei countryside.

Award-winning illustrator Ann Grifalconi shares her vision of the West Indian island of Trinidad in Lynn Joseph's book *Jasmine's Parlour Day*. Young Jasmine helps her mother set up her family's wares of fish and sugar cakes in the wooden parlours used by the islanders to sell goods. Using predominantly pink, purple, and green washes of color, Grifalconi transforms readers into eager island tourists, also partaking of the local wares.

Niki Daly uses pencils and watercolors to illustrate Ingrid Mennen's *One Round Moon and a Star for Me*, a book relating the anxiety felt by a young boy who watches as three young girls help deliver Mama's new baby. Daly vividly captures everyday details of rural South African life.

Expressive watercolor illustrations of the Caribbean by Caroline Binch accompany Rita Mitchell's account of *Hue Boy*, a young boy who fears he will never grow in size. When his father returns from a long shipping trip and they walk hand-in-hand through the village, Hue Boy feels very proud next to his father, which in turn makes him feel very tall. Binch's realistic pictures have a photographic quality to them, also allowing readers to identify with the characters.

POETRY ABOUT FAMILIES

Poetry, too, can help children enjoy and appreciate the diversity of human life, especially when the books are as beautifully illustrated as the titles described below.

Ann Nolan Clark's *In My Mother's House*, illustrated by Velino Herrara, is a 1942 Caldecott Honor Medal book that was reissued in 1991. The Tewa children of Tesuque Pueblo share poetry about their world. Through words and illustrations, one can see pueblo houses built of adobe bricks standing close together around a plaza, mothers grinding corn with grinding stones, fathers tending cornfields, ceremonial dances thanking the sun and rain, and horses and sheep grazing the lands.

Lynn Joseph recounts the daily activities of a young girl in Trinidad through poetry in *Coconut Kind of Day*. With rhythmic poems and swishes of tropical colors, children can experience the smells, sounds, and foods of the island, such as enjoying steel band music, visiting the *palet* man (ice cream man) who sells *soursop* (a fruit) ice cream, and seeing fishermen "pullin' seine" (fishermen gathering on the beach and pulling in the fishing nets).

Four books of poetry that celebrate African American families include: Eloise Greenfield's *Night on Neighborhood Street*, illustrated by Jan Spivey Gilchrist; Wade Hudson's *Pass It On* and Joyce Carol Thomas's *Brown Honey in Broomwheat Tea* both illustrated by Floyd Cooper; and the Strickland's book *Families* illustrated by John Ward. Jan Spivey Gilchrist uses gouache paintings highlighted with pastels to illustrate poems that range in subject matter from an older sister tucking her younger sister into bed, families spending fun time together, a father out of work, and children avoiding a drug dealer. Floyd Cooper uses oil washes on board to accompany poems in the two books he illustrated that center on life and play in African American families.

And, finally, in *Families*, John Ward uses bright acrylics against white and black backdrops in poems that celebrate the diversity of African American families. Among the poets included are Lucille Clifton, Langston Hughes, and Eloise Greenfield. The opening poem in the book is a beautiful tribute to all kinds of families.

BIBLIOGRAPHY

Family history/discovering ancestry

Crews, Donald. *Bigmama's*. New York: Greenwillow, 1991.

———. *Short Cut*. New York: Greenwillow, 1992,

Johnson, Angela. *Tell Me a Story, Mama*. Illustrated by David Soman. New York: Orchard, 1989.

Hoffman, Mary. *Boundless Grace*. Illustrated by Caroline Binch. New York: Dial, 1995.

Pellegrini, Nina. *Families Are Different*. New York: Holiday, 1991.

Say, Allen. *Grandfather's Journey*. Boston, MA: Houghton Mifflin, 1993.

———. *Tree of Cranes*. Boston, MA: Houghton Mifflin, 1991.

Williams, Sherley Anne. *Working Cotton*. Illustrated by Carole Byard. New York: Harcourt, 1992.

Intergenerational stories

Dorros, Arthur. *Isla*. Illustrated by Elisa Kleven. New York: Dutton, 1995.

———. *Abuela*. Illustrated by Elisa Kleven. New York: Dutton, 1991.

Flournoy, Valerie. *Patchwork Quilt*. Illustrated by Jerry Pinkney. New York: Dial, 1985.

———. *Tanya's Reunion*. Illustrated by Jerry Pinkney. New York: Dial, 1995.

Grifalconi, Ann. *Kinda Blue.* New York: Little, Brown, 1993.

———. *Osa's Pride.* New York: Little, Brown, 1990.

———. *The Village of Round and Square Houses.* New York: Little, Brown, 1986.

Guback, Georgia. *Luka's Quilt.* New York: Greenwillow, 1994.

Howard, Elizabeth. *Aunt Flossie's Hats (and Crab Cakes Later).* Illustrated by James Ransome. New York: Clarion, 1991.

Johnson, Angela. *When I Am Old With You.* Illustrated by David Soman. New York: Orchard, 1990.

Linden, Ann Marie. *One Smiling Grandma.* Illustrated by Lynne Russell. New York: Dial, 1992.

Mitchell, Margaree King. *Uncle Jed's Barbershop.* Illustrated by James Ransome. New York: Simon & Schuster, 1993.

Nye, Naomi Shihab. *Sitti's Secrets.* Illustrated by Nancy Carpenter. New York: Four Winds, 1994.

Oberman, Sheldon. *The Always Prayer Shawl.* Illustrated by Ted Lewin. Honesdale, PA: Boyds Mills, 1994.

Pinkney, Gloria Jean. *Back Home.* Illustrated by Jerry Pinkney. New York: Dial, 1992.

———. *Sunday Outing.* Illustrated by Jerry Pinkney. New York: Dial, 1994.

Polacco, Patricia. *Chicken Sunday.* New York: Philomel, 1992.

———. *Mrs. Katz and Tush.* New York: Bantam, 1992.

———. *Pink and Say.* New York: Philomel, 1994.

Stolz, Mary. *Storm in the Night.* Illustrated by Pat Cummings. New York: Harper, 1988.

Family life for children growing up in America with dual cultures

Ancona, George. *Powwow.* New York: Harcourt, 1993.

———. *Earth Daughter.* New York: Simon & Schuster, 1995.

Brown, Tricia. *Hello, Amigos!* Photographs by Fran Ortiz. New York: Holt, 1986.

———. *Lee Ann: The Story of a Vietnamese-American Girl.* Photographs by Ted Thai. New York: Putnam, 1991.

Gordon, Ginger. *My Two Worlds.* Photographs by Martha Cooper. New York: Clarion, 1993.

Heweft, Joan. *Hector Lives in the United States Now.* Photographs by Richard Heweft. New York: Lippincott, 1990.

Hoyt-Goldsmith, Diane. *Cherokee Summer.* Photographs by Lawrence Migdale. New York: Holiday, 1993.

————. *Hoang Anh: A Vietnamese-American Boy.* Photographs by Lawrence Migdale. New York: Holiday, 1992.

Keegan, Marcia. *Pueblo Boy: Growing Up in Two Worlds.* New York: Cobblehill, 1991.

Kendall, Russ. *Eskimo Boy.* New York: Scholastic, 1992.

Kuklin, Susan. *How My Family Lives in America.* New York: Bradbury, 1992.

Thomas, Jane Resh. *Lights on the River.* Illustrated by Michael Dooling. New York: Hyperion, 1994.

Waters, Kate & Madeline Slovenz-Low. *Lion Dancer.* Photographs by Martha Cooper. New York: Scholastic, 1990.

Family life of children from America living in other countries

Binch, Caroline. *Gregory Cool.* New York: Dial, 1994.

Kroll, Virginia. *Masai and I.* New York: Four Winds, 1992.

Leigh, Nila K. *Learning to Swim in Swaziland: A Child's Eye-View of a Southern African Country.* New York: Scholastic, 1993.

Williams, Karen Lynn. *When Africa Was Home.* Illustration by Floyd Cooper. New York: Orchard, 1991.

Family life for children in other countries

Baer, Edith. *This Is the Way We Eat Our Lunch: A Book About Children Around the World.* Illustrated by Steve Bjorkman. New York: Scholastic, 1995.

———— *This Is the Way We Go to School: A Book About Children Around the World.* Illustrated by Steve Bjorkman. New York: Scholastic, 1990.

Dorros, Arthur. *This Is My House.* New York: Scholastic, 1992.

Heide, Florence Parry & Judith Heide Gilliland. *The Day of Ahmed's Secret.* Illustrated by Ted Lewin. New York: Lothrop, 1990.

————. *Sami and the Time of the Troubles.* Illustrated by Ted Lewin. New York: Clarion, 1992.

Isadora, Rachel. *At the Crossroads.* New York: Greenwillow, 1991.

————. *Over the Green Hills.* New York: Greenwillow, 1992.

Joseph, Lynn. *Jasmine's Parlour Day.* Illustrated by Ann Grifalconi. New York: Lothrop, 1994.

Mennen, Ingrid. *One Round Moon and a Star for Me.* Illustrated by Niki Daly. New York: Orchard, 1994.

Mitchell, Rita. *Hue Boy.* Illustrated by Caroline Binch. New York: Dial, 1993.

Morris, Ann. Series of books: *Bread, Bread, Bread; Hats, Hats, Hats; Houses and Homes; Loving; On the Go; Shoes, Shoes, Shoes; Tools;* and *Weddings.* Photographs by Ken Heyman. New York: Lothrop.

Poetry about families

Clark, Ann Nolan. *In My Mother's House.* Illustrated by Velino Herrara. New York: Viking, 1991.

Greenfield, Eloise. *Night on Neighborhood Street.* Illustrated by Jan Spivey Gilchrist. New York: Dial, 1991.

Hudson, Wade, selector. *Pass It On: African-American Poetry for Children.* Illustrated by Floyd Cooper. New York: Scholastic, 1993.

Joseph, Lynn. *Coconut Kind of Day.* Illustrated by Sandra Speidel. New York: Lothrop, 1990.

Strickland, Dorothy S. & Michael R. Strickland, selectors. *Families: Poems Celebrating the African American Experience.* Illustrated by John Ward. Honesdale, PA: Wordsong, 1994.

Thomas, Joyce Carol. *Brown Honey in Broomwheat Tea.* Illustrated by Floyd Cooper. New York: HarperCollins, 1993.

ABOUT THE AUTHOR

Sue McCleaf Nespeca is Youth Services Coordinator for NOLA Regional Library System, a consortium of 90 public, school, academic, and special libraries in northeast Ohio. She is the author of *Library Programming for Families with Young Children* (1994), published by Neal-Schuman, and coauthor of *Programming for Young Children: Birth Through Age Five* (1996), published by the ALA.

Lullabies, Lyrics and Gallows Songs by Christian Morgenstern, illustrated by Lisbeth Zwerger.

14

HOW DO THEY STACK UP?
BEST PICTURE BOOKS FROM ABROAD
MAUREEN WHITE

HOW DO THE BEST picture books from abroad stack up with those from the United States? Those of us who live in the United States believe that we possess the best picture books in the world., We are truly blessed with outstanding authors and illustrators who produce beautifully written and illustrated children's books. But do we have "all" of the best picture books in the world? Poet, author, and translator Naomi Shihab Nye, speaking primarily of translations, gives us her answer to the question: "Those of us living in the U.S. often suffer from a particular literary provinciality, imagining ourselves to be the primary readers and writers of the planet."[1]

In addition to Nye's charge of "literary provinciality," we also need to be aware of the literature of other countries for more positive reasons. In an interview on translations for *Book Links*, translator, linguist, and publisher Dagmar Herrmann provides us with just such a reason: "I believe from a very tender age children ought to be exposed to writers and illustrators around the world—accomplished artists that have already proven themselves abroad… writers with a different view and illustrators with a different touch. Our children only gain; they are enriched."[2]

Some of the best translated picture books from abroad are available through U.S. publishers, so why do we not select these books for our collections? Is there something inherently different or foreign about them that is unappealing to us? The longtime concern of publishers, librarians, and booksellers has been the ability of translated books to "travel well." However, since in picture books there is less emphasis on text, shouldn't well-illustrated books "travel" well?

The original question now needs to be rephrased: How do the best translated children's picture books from abroad and published in the

U.S. compare with the best picture books produced by authors and illustrators from the United States in 1995? What are the differences in these two groups, if any? The year 1995 was the perfect year for me to analyze the similarities and differences in these books. As a member of the 1996 Caldecott Committee, I had access to the best picture books published in the U.S. in 1995. And, as editor for the *USBBY Newsletter* column "How Does That Translate? Best Books from Abroad," the best in translated children's books, including picture books, were made available to me.

Difficulties are inherent when comparing the small number of translated picture books with the large number of books produced by U.S. authors and illustrators. However, the very act of comparing the best produced by different cultures, will hopefully be one of discovery. Marcel Proust said, "The real voyage of discovery consists not in seeking new landscapes but in having new eyes." May the very act of comparing the best of both groups help us to look at translated picture books with new eyes.

It is estimated that each year approximately five thousand children's books are published by U.S. publishers.[3] According to Huck, Hepler, and Hickman, approximately two-thirds of these books are picture books.[4] Horning, Kruse, and Schliesman estimated that of this five thousand, fewer than 199 were translated children's books and that the number was probably closer to 80. Furthermore, they concluded that "children's books translated into English and published by U.S. publishers continue to be very few in number ... [and] most of these children's translated books were picture books."[5]

Editor Margaret McElderry, longtime proponent of the importance of literature from abroad, observed in her 1994 May Hill Arbuthnot Honor Lecture, "... though I don't foresee any rapid increase in translations into English of books for older readers, the exchange of picture books, such an important part of our market here, will of course continue unabated."[6] Data collected by White and Link on 1995 translations support McElderry's observation. They found that of the 69 translated books for children reviewed by major review sources in 1995, 50 of them, or 73 percent, were picture books.[7]

The increased popularity of international picture books was addressed by Andreas Bode, Chief Librarian of the International Youth Library in Munich. He observed that "... the picture book was the prima donna of the international children's book publishing world and that it was experiencing a popularity like no other children's format."[8] The consensus of those who study, review, and edit children's literature is that although the number of books that are translated from other languages into English and published by U.S.

publishers is very small, there seem to be more translated picture books published than purely textual translations.

CALDECOTT BOOKS

To begin our comparison, let us look at the familiar—the Caldecott Award Books. This award is given for distinguished illustrations in a picture book and for excellence of pictorial presentation for children. Other components are considered, such as the blending of the written text with the illustrations and the overall design of the book, but the primary focus is on the illustrations.[9]

The 1996 Caldecott Awards were given to books published in 1995. The Caldecott Medal Book was *Officer Buckle and Gloria*, written and illustrated by Peggy Rathmann. Caldecott Honor Awards went to *Alphabet City*, illustrated by Stephen Johnson; *The Faithful Friend* by Robert D. San Souci, illustrated by Brian Pinkney; *Tops and Bottoms* written and illustrated by Janet Stevens; and *Zin! Zin! Zin! A Violin* by Lloyd Moss, illustrated by Marjorie Priceman.

In each of these Caldecott books we see large, beautiful illustrations composed from a palette of bold, bright colors. The illustrations seem to be right up front; they leap out at the reader. With the exception of *The Faithful Friend*, these Caldecott books contain stories that are not threatening to children. The genres include two books of folklore, two information books, and one humorous work of realistic fiction. Publishers of these books were major publishers in the field of children's books.

Diverse subjects were addressed, including safety, the police and schools, music, the alphabet, friendships, and animals. A variety of media was used by these illustrators. Stevens used watercolor, colored pencils, and gesso in *Tops and Bottoms*. Priceman used gouache in *Zin! Zin! Zin!* and Brian Pinkney used scratchboard and oil in *The Faithful Friend*. Johnson made use of a variety of media in *Alphabet City*. Rathmann's choice of media was watercolor with black line sketches for *Officer Buckle and Gloria*.

The choice of styles for these Caldecott Books was just as varied as the mediums used. Styles included: expressionism in *Zin! Zin! Zin!*; a cartoon style for *Tops and Bottoms* as well as in *Officer Buckle and Gloria*; realism in *Alphabet City*; and, finally, the unique style of Pinkney, created by his scratchboard technique, for *The Faithful Friend*. Each Caldecott Book is unique in style and use of media, yet as a group there is a commonality among them. Perhaps it is in the total bookmanship, the oversized book format, the familiar type faces and the use of bold, bright colors. As beautiful as they are, as a group they all seem to say, "U.S.A., U.S.A."

TRANSLATED PICTURE BOOKS

Before we look at some of the best translated children's picture books from 1995, a review of this less familiar literature might be helpful. The Batchelder Award is a good place to begin. This award is given to U.S. publishers to encourage publication of translations of children's books into English. Criteria exclude books that are "unduly Americanized." Fairy tales as a genre are also excluded. And the Batchelder Award criteria state that "primary attention must be directed to the text... picture books should be considered only if the text is substantial and at least as important as the pictures."[10] Therefore, it becomes the task of each Batchelder Committee to determine if a translated picture book meets this criterion.

In reviewing past Batchelder Award books we find that several picture books have been selected for the award. In 1979, *Rabbit Island,* written by Jorg Steiner and illustrated by Jorg Muller, was selected as the Batchelder Award-winning book. Muller is the 1994 Hans Christian Andersen Award winner for illustrations. In 1983, *Hiroshima No Pika,* written and illustrated by Toshi Maruki, was honored with the award. And, in 1986, *Rose Blanche* by Roberto Innocenti and Christophe Gallaz and illustrated by Innocenti, received the Batchelder Award.

Picture books have also won Batchelder Honor Awards. They include: *Anne Frank: Beyond the Diary: A Photographic Remembrance,* by Rian Verhoeven and Ruud van der Rol, and *The Princess and the Kitchen Garden,* by Annemie and Margriet Heymans, in 1994. In 1996, *Star of Fear, Star of Hope,* by Jo Hoestlandt and illustrated by Johannna Kang, was a Batchelder Honor Book.

Seven selected 1995 translated picture books will be compared as a group to the five 1996 Caldecott Award Books. The selected translated picture books were produced by illustrators from abroad and received either an award, an honor or one or more outstanding reviews from major review sources. These review sources included *Booklist, School Library Journal, Horn Book, The Bulletin for the Center of Children's Books, Kirkus Reviews* and *Publishers Weekly.* You will be introduced to each of these seven books through (a) brief imprint information, (b) a description of the illustrations, and (c) the review or award given to the book.

Anno's Magic Seeds was written and illustrated by Mitsumasa Anno and translated from the Japanese. Anno makes gentle use of watercolor without the use of black pen to give the viewer a feeling of a warm, gentle breath of spring. Each page has a simple watercolor-lined border. Illustrations vary in size: sometimes small, some full-page, and a final double-page illustration. This selection includes ample use of white space and was named as a 1995 *Booklist* Editor's Choice.

Friends Go Adventuring was written and illustrated by Helme Heine and translated from the German. Lively and fresh watercolor illustrations, use of great splashes of color, and double-page spreads exude humor and fun for all. Close attention to imaginative detail and a blend of an impressionistic and an almost cartoon-type style are characteristic of Heine's work. This book received a pointer review from *Kirkus Reviews* and starred reviews in *School Library Journal* and *Publishers Weekly*.

Little Hobbin was written by Theodore Storm and illustrated by Lisbeth Zwerger and translated from the German. Done in delicate watercolor, the elegant borders in the full-page illustrations creatively balance the small illustrations placed on each opposite page of text, all characteristic marks of Zwerger's work. *Booklist* ranked it among Zwerger's best works, and it received a starred review from *Publishers Weekly*. Another unusual book illustrated by Zwerger in 1995 was *Christian Morgenstern: Lullabies, Lyrics and Gallows Songs*.

[October 45]: Childhood Memories of the War was written and illustrated by Jean-Louis Besson and translated from the French. Besson uses a mixture of small, vignette-type illustrations, as well as full-page art, and double-page spreads. The text is done in an unusual font. The medium used was watercolor with black pen. Cartoon artwork provides a safety net for the young reader, making the serious subject of survival accessible to all. This book received a starred review from *Booklist*.

The Red Poppy was written and illustrated by Irmgard Lucht and translated from the German. Lucht presents a larger-than-life perspective of the growth, death, and rebirth of a field of red poppies. Acrylic paintings in this oversized picture book are complemented by large 18-point type. Wise use of white space and vibrant colors, especially the dark greens and striking reds, provide the background for the detailed almost surrealistic work. This book received a starred review in *School Library Journal*.

Shin's Tricycle was written by Tatsuharu Kodama, illustrated by Noriyuki Ando, and translated from the Japanese. Ando makes heavy use of colors from a palette of oranges, yellows, and purples that explode on the page. Mixed full-page art and double-page spreads without borders, an expressionistic style, and paintings heavily textured with a scratching tool describe the illustrations in this picture book meant for older children. It received a starred review in *Booklist* and a pointer review in *Kirkus Reviews*.

Star of Fear, Star of Hope, was written by Jo Hoestlandt, illustrated by Johanna Kang, and translated from the French. The illustrations are subdued and somber in mood. Kang uses full-page, primitive illustrations bordered in off-white, paper doll figures, and sepia tones to point to the fragility of life and the horrors of war in this haunting book. This selection received the 1996 Batchelder Honor Award, was the winner of the 1994 Bologna Book Fair Graphics Prize, and was an ALA Notable Book.

How can we describe this group of seven acclaimed translated picture books? First, consider the languages: three books were German translations, two were Japanese, and two were French. The artistic medium of choice was watercolor, with five of the seven choosing this medium. The style varied among the seven illustrators. Styles range from the cartoon art of *{October 45}*, to the impressionistic style of *Anno's Magic Seed*, to the expressionistic art of *Shin's Tricycle*. A naive, primitive folk style was used in *Star of Fear, Star of Hope* and the impressionistic style by Heine in *Friends Go Adventuring*. Lucht uses realistic art to illustrate *The Red Poppy*, but it appears to be almost surrealistic to the U.S. viewer. Zwerger has her own unique style, which is difficult to label. Translated genres include one work of historical fiction, three information books, two fantasies, and one biography. World War II was the subject of three of these books. Four of the seven translated picture books analyzed were published by smaller publishers that often publish translations, while the other three were published by major publishers.

CONCLUSIONS

What are the differences that can be observed between these translated books from abroad and the Caldecott Books? One difference seems to be in the size of the illustrations, with smaller illustrations and more attention given to the tiny details in the translated books. These illustrations were gentle, smaller, not "up front, in your face," as in the Caldecott Books. With the exception of *The Red Poppy* and *Shin's Tricycle*, the artwork is almost understated. Unfamiliar or unusual fonts and type sizes are sometimes used in translations. For example, an extra large, 18-point type was used in *The Red Poppy* and an unusually small, odd type was used in *{October 45}*. While there seems to be a greater diversity of artistic styles used in translations, the Caldecott books made more varied use of media than did translations. Translated books may seem odd, unusual, almost surrealistic to

U.S. viewers. Because translations are from a variety of countries and cultures, there seems to be a greater diversity in illustrations, style, size, and typeface that does create a different-looking book.

Also, consider the difference in the subjects of translated picture books. There is a greater use of serious subjects in these stories. World War II was the subject in three of the seven translated picture books, a subject not found in the Caldecott Books, or often found in other children's books from the States.

When the selected translated picture books were shared with groups of literature-wise, second-grade elementary school students, their reactions included "cool," "wow," "It is so sad," and "Where are the Spanish translations?" These were very perceptive comments and questions from young children. Many of these children had previously checked out eye-catching books such as *The Red Poppy, Star of Fear, Star of Hope,* and *Shin's Tricycle.* None of these students were aware that the books were translations. A group of sixth graders devoured *{October 45},* again not knowing it was a translation. They seemed intrigued with the artistic presentation of the subject of survival in World War II.

Consider the question of that second grader, "Where are the Spanish translations?" A recent study of translated books shows that most of our translations still come from the European languages of German and French, with a steady increase in Japanese translations.[11] In addition to the lack of translations of books originally written in Spanish, Thelma Seto calls for more translations from non-European languages. In an article for *Horn Book,* "Multiculturalism is Not Halloween," she declared "… non-Euro-American writers have not yet broken into the children's literature market … we are out there … it would be far more fruitful for publishers to seek out translators who might bring to American children the literature of other cultures and nations."[12]

Where does one find outstanding translated picture books? Major publishers continue to publish several translated books each year. However, many smaller publishers such as Front Street, Wellington, and Kane/Miller are actively publishing translations. Translated picture books from the German language are often published by North-South Books, which has a direct connection to the book industry in Switzerland. Many Swedish translations are published by R & S Books, affiliated with Farrar, Straus and Giroux.[13]

Although this comparison of a group of translated children's books with Caldecott books addresses only the books published in one year, what we have considered are perceptions—perceptions of what is outstanding, what the illustrator is saying through the pictures, what will be accepted by the reader in the States, and what will sell. You are encouraged to select translated picture books for their literary and artistic quality, as well as for their differences. If we do not select for literary and artistic quality, we will only perpetuate the myth that these books do not "travel well." Let us not be guilty of excluding translated picture books from our collections because they are different. First, select them if they are outstanding, and second, select them because they will introduce our boys and girls to that which is different in a visually appealing way.

How do they stack up? Perhaps our questions should be, "What will we miss if we exclude these books from abroad from our collections?" Hazel Rochman, writing about her earlier years in South Africa and the literature from other cultures, answered it best in *Against Borders*. "I was blind, and I was frightened. I was shut in. And I was denied access to the stories and music of the world."[14] Let us not be blind, deny or be denied the best stories and children's picture books from other languages.

Notes

1. *This Same Sky: A Collection of Poems from around the World,* selected by Naomi Shihab Nye. New York: Four Winds, 1992, p. xii.

2. "Talking Translations: An Interview with Dagmar Herrmann," *Book Links.* January 1994, V. 3, No. 3, p. 40-41.

3. Bernice E. Cullinan and Lee Galda, *Literature and the Child,* 1994, 3rd ed. Fort Worth, TX: Harcourt Brace College Publishers, p. xii.

4. Charlotte S. Huck, Susan Hepler, Janet Hickman, *Children's Literature in the Elementary School,* 1994, 5th ed. Fort Worth, TX: Harcourt Brace College Publishers, p. 155.

5. Kathleen T. Horning, Ginny Moore Kruse and Megan Schliesman. Madison, WI: *CCBC Choices 1994, 1995, Friends of the CCBC,* Inc., p. 9.

6. Margaret K. McElderry, "Across the Years, Across the Seas: Notes from an Errant Editor," *Journal of Youth Services in Libraries,* Summer 1994, V. 7, No. 4, p. 379.

7. Unpublished data on 1995 translated children's picture books collected by Maureen White and Susan Link.

8. Andreas Bode, "Text Illustration: An Endangered Art Form?" *Bookbird: World of Children's Books,* Winter 1994, V. 32, No. 4, p. 8.

9. Caldecott Award criteria were adopted by the ALSC Board, January 1978 and revised Midwinter, 1987.

10. Batchelder Award criteria were adopted by the ALSC Board, Annual Conference 1981, revised Midwinter, 1987.

11. Maureen White and Susan Link in a presentation, "Is it Danish, Dutch, French, German ... Or Does It Really Matter Anymore?: Chil-

dren's Literature Transfer Via Translation," at the 5th Conference of Librarians in International Development, Kansas City, May 1, 1995.

12. Thelma Seto, "Multiculturalism Is Not Halloween," *The Horn Book Magazine*, March/April 1995, V. 71, No. 2, p. 172.

13. Horning, Kruse and Schliesman, *CCBC Choices* 1994, p. 9.

14. Hazel Rochman, "Against Borders," *The Horn Book Magazine*, March/April 1995, V. 71, No. 2, p. 156.

WORKS CITED

1995 Caldecott Books

Johnson, Stephen T. *Alphabet City*. New York: Viking, 1995.

Moss, Lloyd. *Zin! Zin! Zin! A Violin*. Illustrated by Marjorie Priceman. New York: Simon & Schuster, 1995.

Rathmann, Peggy. *Officer Buckle and Gloria*. New York: Putnam, 1995.

San Souci, Robert D. *The Faithful Friend*. Illustrated by Brian Pinkney. New York: Simon & Schuster, 1995.

Stevens, Janet. *Tops and Bottoms*. New York: Harcourt, 1995.

Translated picture books

Anno, Mitsumasa. *Anno's Magic Seeds*. Translated from the Japanese. New York: Philomel, 1995.

Besson, Jean-Louis. *{October 45}: Childhood Memories of the War*. Translated from the French by Carol Volk. New York: Creative Editions. Harcourt, 1995.

Christian Morgenstern: Lullabies, Lyrics and Gallows Songs. Selected and illustrated by Lisbeth Zwerger. Translated from the German by Anthea Bell. New York: North-South, 1995.

Heymans, Annemie and Margriet Heymans. *The Princess in the Kitchen Garden*. Translated from the Dutch by Johanna H. and Johanna W. Prins. New York: Farrar, Straus & Giroux, 1993.

Heine, Helme. *Friends Go Adventuring*. Translated from the German. New York: McElderry, 1995.

Hoestlandt, Jo. *Star of Fear, Star of Hope*. Illustrated by Johanna Kang. Translated from the French by Mark Polizzotti. New York: Walker, 1995.

Innocenti, Roberto and Christophe Gallaz. *Rose Blanche*. Illustrated by Roberto Innocenti. Translated by Martha Coventry and Richard Graglia. Mankato, MN: Creative Education, 1985.

Kodama, Tatsuharu. *Shin's Tricycle*. Illustrated by Noriyuki Ando. Translated from the Japanese by Kazuko Hokumen-Jones. New York: Walker, 1995.

Lucht, Irmgard. *The Red Poppy.* Translated from the German by Frank Jocoby-Nelson. New York: Hyperion, 1995.

Maruki, Toshi. *Hiroshima No Pika.* Translated from the Japanese. New York: Lothrop, 1982.

Steiner, Jorg. *Rabbit Island.* Illustrated by Jorg Muller. Translated from the German by Ann Conrad Lammers. New York: Bergh, 1978.

Storm, Theodor. *Little Hobbin.* Illustrated by Lisbeth Zwerger. Translated from the German by Anthea Bell. New York: North-South, 1995.

Verhoeven, Rian and Ruud van der Rol. *Anne Frank: Beyond the Diary: A Photographic Remembrance.* Translated from the Dutch by Tony Langham and Plym Petters. New York: Viking, 1993.

Selected bibliography of other translated picture books for children

Andersen, Hans Christian. *Twelve Tales.* Illustrated and translated from the Danish by Erik Blegvad. New York: McElderry/Macmillan, 1994.

Bjork, Christina. *Big Bear's Book by Himself.* Illustrated by Inga-Karin Eriksson. Translated from the Swedish by Joan Sandin. New York: R & S Books, 1993.

Buchholtz, Quint. *Sleep Well, Little Bear.* Translated from the German by Peter F. Neumeyer. New York: Farrar, Straus & Giroux, 1994.

I Dream of Peace: Images of War by Children of Former Yugoslavia. Illustrations by the children. Translated by UNICEF translators. New York: HarperCollins, 1994.

Kharms, Daniil. *The Story of a Boy Named Will Who Went Sledding Down the Hill.* Illustrated by Vladimir Radunsky. Translated from the Russian by James Gambrell. New York: North-South, 1993.

Landstrom, Olof and Lena Landstrom. *Will Goes to the Post Office.* Translated from the Swedish by Elisabeth Dyssegaard. New York: R & S Books, 1994. See also *Will Goes to the Beach,* 1995; *Will's New Cap,* 1992; and *Will Gets a Haircut,* 1993, all R & S Books.

Levine, Arthur A. *On Cat Mountain.* Illustrated by Anne Buguet. Adapted from a French translation by Francois Richard. New York: Putnam, 1994.

Mado, Michio. *The Animals.* Illustrated by Mitsumasa Anno. Translated from the Japanese by The Empress Michiko of Japan. New York: McElderry, 1992.

Pfister, Marcus. *The Christmas Star.* Translated from the German by J. Alison James. New York: North-South, 1993.

———. *The Rainbow Fish.* Translated from the German by J. Alison James. New York: North-South, 1992.

Ruepp, Krista. *Midnight Rider.* Illustrated by Ulrike Heyne. Translated from the German by J. Alison James. New York: North-South, 1995.

Scheffler, Ursel. *Rinaldo on the Run.* Illustrated by Iskender Gider. Translated from the German by J. Alison James. New York: North-South, 1995. See also *Rinaldo, the Sly Fox*, 1992 and *The Return of Rinaldo, the Sly Fox*, 1993, all North-South.

Skira-Venturi, Rosabianca. *A Weekend with Leonardo da Vinci.* Translated from the French by Ann Keay Beneduce. New York: Rizzoli, 1993. See also *A Weekend with Degas*, 1991; *A Weekend with Picasso*, 1991; *A Weekend with Rembrandt*, 1992; *A Weekend Velazquez*, 1993; and *A Weekend with Matisse*, 1994, all Rizzoli.

ABOUT THE AUTHOR

Maureen White is Assistant Professor of Education at the University of Houston-Clear Lake, where she teaches children's and young adult literature. She served on the 1996 Caldecott Award Committee and on the 1992 Batchelder Award Committee for the Association for Library Service to Children. She received the 1990 Beta Phi Mu Harold Lancour Foreign Study Scholarship for further study of children's literature in England and Germany. Her research, publications, and presentations continue to focus on children's books translated from other languages into English. This interest stems from her dissertation research for the Ph.D. at Texas Woman's University, 1990, on the study of successful translated children's books.

APPENDIX A

A LISTING OF SELECTED MULTICULTURAL TRADE BOOKS FOR CHILDREN AND YOUNG ADULTS

EDITED BY IONE COWEN

IN THE FOLLOWING bibliography, we have tried to represent the increasingly broad understanding of multiculturalism as portrayed through the art in children's and young adult books. Members of the Virginia Hamilton Advisory Board, which is composed of teachers, school library media specialists and children's librarians in public libraries, were invited to submit titles of merit which they had found useful in blending the art and the story. They were requested to focus on books they had successfully utilized in their own teaching, story-telling and many other experiences in their work with children and young adults. The books were selected for their authentic representation of the culture and their appropriateness for the interest level. The following titles are recommended for purchase in public libraries and school library media centers.

All entries are coded for their interest level with a letter code following the date. K-Kindergarten; P-Primary; I-Intermediate; J-Junior High; S-Senior High.

> Adoff, Arnold. *In for Winter, Out for Spring.* Illustrated by Jerry Pinkney. New York: Harcourt, 1991. (K-I-P)
>
> Poems and pictures chronicle a year in the life of young, vivacious Rebecca as she moves through the seasons and experiences nature's abundant wonders with the support of her caring family. Adoff's precise, energetic poems and Pinkney's vigorous, dramatic watercolors work in tandem to evoke an extraordinary sense of a rural setting and to crystallize a wide range of impressions and sensations. Indoors or out and in every season, Rebecca makes discoveries which encourage children and their older allies to observe and respect those awesome happenings that unfold daily in the natural world.

————. *Slow Dance Heartbreak Blues.* Illustrated by William Cotton. New York: Lothrop, 1995. (J-S)

As though inspired by the hard-driven rhythms of rock music and the soulful, sinewy twists and turns of jazz lyrics, Adoff serves up a cycle of highly charged poems that reveals some of the pains, perils, and pleasures of adolescence. Through the voices of his young narrators—a sensitive, candid, achingly cynical, and ultimately hopeful lot—he probes questions and concerns about identity, relationships, social issues, and matters of the heart and spirit. Off-beat, intriguing black and white photographs rendered in the manner of abstract collages plumb the moods and emotions the poems evoke.

Angelou, Maya. *My Painted House, My Friendly Chicken & Me.* New York: Crown, 1994. (I-J)

Poet Maya Angelou tells the story of Thandi, a Ndebele girl from a village in South Africa. As Thandi describes her village the reader becomes aware that although the traditional culture predominates, touches of modern life are beginning to be felt. The book's design incorporates different sizes of type as words and photographs are intermingled to add emphasis to the story. The unusual placement of text and pictures, combined with the use of background colors alternating with white pages, produces a unique setting for the child's narrative.

Bartone, Elisa. *Peppe the Lamplighter.* Illustrated by Ted Lewin. New York: Lothrop, 1993. (P-I)

Set in New York City's Little Italy at the turn of the century, a young boy named Peppe looks for work and finds a job as a lamplighter. His father is disgruntled because this is not the kind of job he had imagined for his only son when he made sacrifices to move his family here in search of the American Dream. Peppe's father soon realizes that Peppe's job as a lamplighter is important when he lights the lamps one dark evening so his little sister, Assunta, will find the way home. Ted Lewin's softly glowing, lamp-lit paintings provide a unique look at city streets and into the home of this immigrant family. A Caldecott Honor Award Book.

Begay, Shonto. *Navajo: Visions and Voices Across the Mesa.* New York: Scholastic, 1995. (P-I-J)

Addressing people outside his culture who wonder "what it means to be an Indian, a Navajo, a Dineh child," Shonto Begay provides striking glimpses of his people, their beliefs, and the challenges they face as they struggle to reconcile past and present by balancing ancient tenets and contemporary values. In twenty lustrous paintings that capture the mysticism inherent in landscape, ceremony, and ritual and an equal number of lissome poems, Begay celebrates the power of spiritual teachings preserved in chants and stories, evokes poignant memories of family, friends, and community, laments the losses and humiliation caused by forced assimilation and summons the voices of elders who admonish the Navajos to protect the earth and who stress the importance of maintaining harmony within. Art and poetry enlighten and engender respect for a fascinating, complex people and their inspiring beliefs. Begay's opening commentary on the ancient and contemporary Navajo world and his place in it establishes the honest, hopeful tone that resounds throughout the entire collection. Notes on the paintings are included.

Bradby, Marie. *More than Anything Else.* Illustrated by Chris K. Soentpiet. New York: Orchard, 1995. (P-I)

Based on the childhood of nine-year-old Booker T. Washington, this story relates his strong desire to learn to read though he works with his father and his brother every day in the salt mines and lives a life of community poverty. Finally, young Booker finds someone to teach him how to make letters and he begins his own journey to the freedom that reading brings to life. A moving story that sets the foundation for Booker's life in the field of education and his own prominent place in history. Watercolor portraits by Soentpiet present settings from the darkened salt mines to the lamplit cabin of Booker's parents.

Bruchac, Joseph and Gayle Ross. *The Girl Who Married the Moon: Stories from Native North America.* New York: BridgeWater, 1994. (I-J)

Organized in four sections to represent four different regions of native North America and sixteen different native nations, the traditional tales in this landmark collection depict the struggles and triumphs of girls and women as they move from innocence to experience and awaken to their powers. Gracefully and eloquently written, the tales abound in tests of endurance, spiritual and physical transformations, sacred rituals and ceremonies, confrontations with ogres from the spirit world, and stormy quests that lead to personal epiphanies. Introductory material and endnotes provide fascinating facts about culture, geographic context, the role of women in traditional native societies, and variants and sources of the tales. The black and white drawing that precedes each section offers a compelling, cameo-like interpretation of significant characters, incidents, and symbols from the tales. Pair this collection with Hamilton's *Her Stories* (Scholastic, 1995).

Bunting, Eve. *Smoky Night.* Illustrated by David Diaz. New York: Harcourt, 1994. (P-I)

During the Los Angeles riots, as Daniel and his mother look out of their window at the smoky night below, they see looters removing goods from neighborhood shops and fires in the distance. When they are forced to leave their apartment and go to a shelter, Daniel is reunited with his lost cat and they both learn the value of getting along with others—no matter what their background or nationality. Collage and acrylic paintings capture the horror of an urban riot while providing hope for a better future.

Chocolate, Debbi. *Kente Colors.* Illustrated by John Ward. New York: Walker, 1996. (P-I)

The author utilizes a simple rhyme to explain Kente patterns. Actual Kente patterns are combined with elaborate depictions of the events they represent. The book reveals that there is much more to Kente than a current fashion statement. It concludes with a brief "Author's Narrative" in which she puts Kente into a historical perspective and shares some of the techniques by which it is made.

Coleman, Evelyn. *White Socks Only.* Illustrated by Tyrone Geter. Morton Grove, IL: Albert Whitman, 1996. (P-I)

Racism, and its by-product segregation, are successfully challenged by an innocent young girl. Guided by an inquisitive nature and unencumbered by the learned roles of the day, she acts in accordance with her personal sense of logic and unwittingly violates social norms. Her unintended act of defiance energizes others to overcome their fears and directly challenge an aspect of inequality. In this particular instance, they prevail with the suggestion that the most vigorous defender of the status quo is punished by a force from within the victim community.

Delacre, Lulu. *Golden Tales.* New York: Scholastic, 1996. (I-J-S)

This handsomely designed treasury of a dozen engaging myths, legends, and folktales from numerous Latin American countries pulsates with cultural authenticity and a deep respect for the lore, land, and history of native peoples who inhabited the Americas when the Spaniards arrived in the late fifteenth century. Focusing on the art, artifacts, and stories of the Taino, Zapotec, Muisca, and Inca tribes, Delacre plies pen and brush to fathom colorful and complex traditions and to reveal the cultural changes that transpired with the blending of native and Spanish customs, values, and religious practices. An introduction includes a map of current Latin American countries, color coded to highlight regions occupied by the four tribes, and a brief history of Latin America. Preceding each of the four sections into which the stories have been placed is an informative overview of the respective cultures. The stories themselves tell of powerful love, of conquest and survival, of the origins of natural wonders and of mystery, magic and miracle. Throughout the book, vibrant full-color oil paintings of dramatic incidents and linocuts of traditional design motifs reveal many cultural details. This entertaining and illuminating collection concludes with notes on sources, extensive explanations of the details and symbols in the stories and artwork, and descriptions of the author/artist's exhaustive research and artistic process. A pronunciation guide is appended.

Doorley, Norah. *Everybody Cooks Rice.* Illustrated by Peter Thornton. Minneapolis, MN: Carolrhoda, 1991. (P)

A young girl searches for her wandering brother for supper, visits several neighbors and is introduced to their cultures as she tastes the various rice dishes they are preparing. The story includes Puerto Rico, India, China, Vietnam, Barbados and Haiti; also recipes.

Feelings, Tom. *The Middle Passage.* New York: Dial, 1995. (I-J)

While the Atlantic slave trade can remain a cold, indifferent fact in the pages of a history textbook, in *The Middle Passage* it becomes a painfully real human tragedy that victimized an estimated thirty to sixty million African men, women, and children for nearly four hundred years. In 64 wrenching black and white narrative paintings, Feelings uncompromisingly lays out a monstrously heinous ordeal of abduction, violence, disease and death. Using muted tones that give this hideous drama the look and feel of a living nightmare, the artist traces a horrific journey of forced migration from village, community and freedom to foreign slave market, which in turn, led the way to a life of immeasurable degradation. While these images of unrelenting suffering linger in the mind long after the book is closed, so does the artist's final impression of human dignity and resilience. Included are Feelings' poignant commentary on the project's evolution and John Henrik Clarke's impassioned account of the politics and history of the slave trade and its long-lasting impact on the social, psychological and economic well-being of African Americans. A map of the African diaspora in the Americas is appended.

———. *Soul Looks Back in Wonder.* New York: Dell, 1994. (I-J)

A collection of poems by a number of leading African American poets, including Langston Hughes, Maya Angelou, and Margaret Walker, that convey the diversity of the African American experience. These poems are intended by the authors to pass on a heritage of strength and endurance, beauty and love, and knowledge and creativity. The text is stunningly illustrated.

Fleming, Virginia. *Be Good to Eddie Lee.* Illustrated by Floyd Cooper. New York: Putnam, 1993. (P-I)

When Christy, JimBud and Eddie Lee go to explore the woods around their neighborhood, it is the latter who proves to be the most observant as he points out details of his surroundings.

Although Christy is initially reluctant to include Eddie Lee because of his Down's syndrome, she comes to appreciate his unique gifts. The oil paintings capture the beauty of nature as seen through the eyes of the children. The full-page illustrations seem to glow with sunlight filtered through the green woods and reflected in a hidden pond. Eddie Lee is realistically portrayed in both text and illustration in this sensitive examination of a special child.

Giovanni, Nikki. *The Genie in the Jar.* Illustrated by Chris Raschka. New York: Henry Holt, 1996. (K-P)

Spinning her words into beautiful images of black songs and black looms, Giovanni inspires us all to trust our hearts in building hope and strength in this hymn to the power of art and love. India ink and watercolor illustrations capture the independent spirit of the young girl as she dances with her mother who is always nearby to protect and guide her.

Greenfield, Eloise. *William & the Good Old Days.* Illustrated by Jan Spivey Gilchrist. New York: HarperCollins, 1993. (P)

A moving story that describes the relationship that William and Grandma used to have until she became ill. William remembers the good times he and Grandma had together, including the time when she had her own restaurant, Mama's Kitchen. William is both angry and sad as he tries to deal with an illness that affects the whole family. A poignant look at how a child struggles to accept and adapt to a major change in their way of life. Gilchrist provides an honest look at a family going through a trying time.

Grimes, Nikki. *C is for City.* Illustrated by Pat Cummings. New York: Lothrop, 1995. (K-P)

An easy-to-read and meticulously painted rhyming verse book. Each letter of the alphabet describes different aspects of life in a city, which will help enable children to identify with the events that are depicted throughout this story. Children will be intrigued by the intensity of the art and the power of the illustrations.

Guback, Georgia. *Luka's Quilt.* New York: Greenwillow, 1994. (K-P)

Luka's excitement over her grandmother's gift of a quilt is dashed when she finds that the colorful garden quilt she imagined is only a traditional two-color Hawaiian quilt. It takes a wonderful spark of ingenuity on Tutu's part to come up with an inspiring idea that saves the day and brings Luke and Tutu together as best friends once again. Bright cut-paper collage illustrations bring the vibrant Hawaiian colors to life.

Hamanaka, Sheila. *The Journey.* New York: Orchard, 1990. (I-J)

Hamanaka chronicles the experience of Japanese Americans who were interned in the U. S. during World War II. The widespread fear and mistrust of Japanese immigrants and Japanese

Myers, Walter Dean. *Brown Angels.* New York: HarperCollins, 1993. (K-P)

> In this wonderful book Walter Dean Myers shares with the reader both the antique photographs of African American children which he collects and his own feelings in a way much more intimate than in his novels. In the introduction Myers confesses unashamedly his love for children and tells how it found action in his searches through "dusty bins in antique shops, flea markets, auction houses and museum collections." We do not know who these children are; their stories are lost with their names. The record of their existence was relegated to the recesses of the antique storages where Myers found them. Each one, however, lives anew as they are loved and experienced by a whole new audience. This is Myers' purpose because he knows that each of the children, some dressed in their very best clothes, was loved and cherished by parents who managed to find the resources to have the pictures taken. Myers also pays tribute to the delight and beauty which the photographer used to preserve the child. Myers hopes that our delight with the pictures—and his warm poems—will cause us both to celebrate our own children and preserve our own stories.

———. *One More River to Cross: An African American Photograph Album.* New York: Harcourt, 1996. (I-J-S)

> Few aspects of African American history go unnoticed in this arresting and eye-opening chronicle of the struggles and achievements of black Americans over the last hundred and fifty years. Using a minimal, poetic narrative and well over one hundred evocative black and white photographs from archives throughout this country and from his own private collection, Myers documents the obstacles, victories, and contributions of a determined, diverse, and often defiant people. What emerges is a candid, eloquent, and respectful portrait of a complex culture. While Myers gives some attention to injustice, bigotry, and survival, he also celebrates the lives of ordinary folks and the remarkable discoveries and successes of many distinguished professionals.

———. *The Story of the Three Kingdoms.* Illustrated by Ashley Bryan. New York: HarperCollins, 1995. (P)

> *The Story of the Three Kingdoms* is an easy reading book. Children will be able to predict what will happen next throughout the story. It is about three kingdoms and the animals who feel they rule these kingdoms. The elephant is the ruler of the forest, the shark is the ruler of the sea and the hawk is the ruler of the sky. The animals learn a valuable lesson in the story—it's not important what you have but how you share it.

Pinkney, Brian. *Max Found Two Sticks.* New York: Simon & Schuster, 1994. (K-P)

A young boy experiences the joys of making music through sounds that he sees and hears around the neighborhood. He creates beautiful music by playing rhythms with two found twigs on various objects.

Polacco, Patricia. *Pink and Say.* New York: Putnam, 1994. (P-I)

Polacco's touching illustrations accompany another of her stories based on family remembrances. Stark white backgrounds create a backdrop for the predominately earth tone watercolors with occasional swatches of bright color used to tell the serious story of two boys' friendship during the Civil War. Pink is African American and Say is Caucasian and both are fighting for the Union army, though Say is afraid to continue fighting the battle for a cause which has so much significance for Pink. The story is definitely a tear-jerker. Pink and Say are captured and taken to Andersonville, where Pink is immediately hanged. Only Say lives to tell the story to his descendants. Polacco wrings emotion from her dramatic illustrations and includes real photographs of her family members to make the story even more believable.

Pollock, Penny. *The Turkey Girl: a Zuni Cinderella.* Illustrated by Ed Young. New York: Little, Brown, 1995. (P-I)

In this thought-provoking Native American version of the familiar Cinderella story, some turkeys make a doeskin dress for the poor girl who tends them so that she can participate in a sacred dance, only to desert her when she fails to return at the promised time. Pastel and oil crayon drawings perfectly capture the vivid colors of the American Southwest and the drama of this story about humankind's bond to nature.

Raschka, Chris. *Charlie Parker Played BeBop.* New York: Orchard, 1992. (K-P)

Though this book appears to be a picture book for young children, it will best be appreciated by adults or older children who understand bebop music and know the importance of Charlie Parker's contribution to the music world. Charlie Parker was an African American alto saxophonist known for his jazz music, and particularly for the rise of bebop, a complex rhythmic form of jazz with many subtle changes of harmony. Without this knowledge, the brilliance of Chris Raschka's illustration will be lost. Raschka is not only an artist and writer, but at one time was a gifted musician. (Tendinitis prevents him from playing viola today.) The design of the book is particularly unique, and even the typeface was selected to convey the feel of bebop. Words, line and motifs repeat, with sheer nonsense intermingled, making the text reflect scat music. The illustrations are full of energy, with repeated motifs of shoes strutting on bird's feet (an inside joke since Charlie Parker was known as "the bird."). The book is fun and can even be used in art or music classes with older students.

Ringgold, Faith. *My Dream of Martin Luther King.* New York: Crown, 1995. (K-P)

Faith Ringgold brings her unique artistic style to this story of Martin Luther King, Jr. Through the telling of her own dream, she relates the story of the civil rights leader and the pursuit of a vision of a better world. Her distinctive artwork is framed by colored borders which vary from page to page. This powerful work shows painful images of police attacking peaceful demonstrators as well as pictures of King with his parents, his wife and children. The use of pastel borders against the predominately black and white illustrations stands in contrast to the harsh reality of discrimination and injustice.

Rochelle, Belinda. *When Jo Louis Won the Title.* Illustrated by Larry Johnson. New York: Houghton Mifflin, 1994. (P-I)

Jo Louis is sitting on her porch wearing a sad face about being the new girl in a new school. When her grandpa comes along and sees her sad face, he cuts through all of her excuses rightly deducing that it is actually her different name and the reaction at the new school that is causing the long, sad face. Grandpa tells Jo the special reason behind her name (which only includes Joe Louis, the boxer) and Jo realizes that every name has its own special story. The next day at the new school she is prepared to talk about her name. This story is lovely, highlighting the relationship between the young girl and her grandfather. The illustrator, a *Boston Globe* editorial sports cartoonist and young adult minister, perfectly implements the story with warm, washed exuberant portraits painted with wide brush strokes. There is intensity on the faces, a zoom-out portrait as the story of long ago begins and an enthusiastic depiction of Harlem the night Joe Louis won the title.

San Souci, Robert D. *The Faithful Friend.* Illustrated by Brian Pinkney. New York: Simon & Schuster, 1995. (P-I)

A retelling of the traditional tale from the French West Indies drawn from African, European and South American tradition in which two friends, Clement and Hippolyte, encounter love, zombies, and danger on the island of Martinique. The story of romance, intrigue, and friendship comes to life through Pinkney's scratchboard and oil illustrations. A Caldecott Honor Book and a Coretta Scott King Honor Illustration Award winner. A glossary with pronunciations is included, and San Souci provides an afterword with background information about the tale.

Say, Allen. *Grandfather's Journey.* New York: Houghton Mifflin, 1993. (K-P-I)

Dramatic single-page paintings accompany a biographical account of Say's grandfather and his own personal experiences of being in love with two different countries, Japan and the United States. While in one country, the protagonists miss the other country and have a yearning to return. Each picture appears as a photograph from a family picture album and the book can be used successfully with family history units or in showing how families bridge two cultures. The striking illustrations won the author/illustrator the coveted Caldecott Medal.

Schroeder, Alan. *Minty: A Story of Young Harriet Tubman.* Illustrated by Jerry Pinkney. New York: Dial, 1996. (P-I)

The young Harriet Tubman was a stubborn and headstrong young girl living on the Brodas plantation in the late 1820s who went by the childhood name of "Minty." The dream of escaping from slavery and living a life of freedom made her life bearable. This collaboration of Schroeder and Pinkney provides readers a glimpse of the young Harriet Tubman that they know as one of America's most famous women for her tireless hard work on the Underground Railroad. Pinkney's pencil, colored pencil and watercolor illustrations reproduced in a larger format provide an incredibly beautiful setting for the story. A preface explains that though this work is a fictional account of Harriet Tubman's childhood, the basic facts are true. An author's note in the back, highlighted will several quotes, gives a brief account of Harriet Tubman's work as an adult.

———. *Satchmo's Blues.* Illustrated by Floyd Cooper. New York: Doubleday, 1996. (P)

On hot summer nights in New Orleans, a boy named Louis Armstrong would peek under the big swinging doors of Economy Hall, listening to the jazz band and dreaming of the day when he would be able to set the stars spinning while blowing his horn. His determination to own his own horn is evident as he works tirelessly to earn the five dollars needed for the purchase of a horn from a neighborhood pawnshop. Cooper's glowing illustrations add depth to this most remarkable story of a young man on his way to becoming the one and only Satchmo, the Ambassador of Jazz.

Soto, Gary. *Chato's Kitchen.* Illustrated by Susan Guevara. New York: Putnam, 1995. (K-P)

Chato the coolest cat in his East L.A. barrio can't believe his good fortune when new neighbors (a family of plump and juicy "ratoncitos," little mice) move in next door. All Chato can think about is how to get them over to his house so he can tempt them with a feast of good food: fajitas, frijoles, salsa, and enchildas. Of course, the main dish will be the guests of honor, who outsmart Chato by bringing along a friend—a dog. A glossary of Spanish words and of Chato's menu are included. Guevara's illustrations provide a lively, colorful setting.

Sullivan, Charles. *Children of Promise: African-American Literature & Art for Young People.* New York: Abrams, 1991. (I-J)

An anthology that chronicles the African American experience in the United States. The reality of African Americans, from the American Revolution to the present day, is examined. The book is composed of excerpts from letters, articles, poems, speeches and other writings, from viewpoints of both African Americans and their oppressors. The photographs and paintings along with the text illustrate the pride and difficulties that African Americans have experienced pursuing the American ideal of freedom and equality.

Wahl, Jan. *Little Eight John.* Illustrated by Wil Clay. New York: Dutton, 1992. (P)

Wil Clay catches the mischievousness of Little Eight John, a boy "who was as mean as mean there was." He purposely disobeys his mother's admonitions, even when his behavior brings illness and misfortune to the family. The brightly colored acrylic paintings show the impish delight the young boy feels, until at last he comes face to face with the very demon about which he has been warned. The use of inset pictures gives an additional dimension to the tale of cause and effect. Different perspectives and visual effects combine to extend the text of this variant of a traditional tale.

Williams, Shirley. *Working Cotton.* Illustrated by Carole Byard. New York: Harcourt, 1992. (K-P)

Acrylic paints were used by award-winning illustrator Carole Byard to depict the life of an African American migrant family picking cotton in California. The story, based on poems written by the author, is told through the youngest family member, Shelan, who is too small to carry her own sack, but is anxious to be as old as her sisters and pick 50 pounds of cotton a day. The pictures are particularly striking when showing the family gathering around a smoky fire in the hazy early morning hours and later in the day as the sweat beads on the faces of family members toiling in the hot sun. The illustrations evoke strong feelings of the tortuous life of migrant laborers.

Williams, Vera B. *Scooter.* New York: Greenwillow, 1993. (I-J)

Elana Rose Rosen needs time to become accustomed to her new apartment in New York City. Obviously, this spirited child will not be idle nor friendless for long as she and her beloved blue scooter take on their new surroundings. The emphasis of text and illustration is on the characters with Elana taking center stage. The margins of almost every page are embellished with pen-and-ink sketches that extend and complement the text in a variety of ways. Acrostics, rows of buttons, spools of thread, lists and tire tracks that resemble zippers add detail and exuberance to this unusual chapter book.

APPENDIX B

A MULTICULTURAL MEDIA FESTIVAL

COMPILED AND EDITED BY CAROLYN S. BRODIE AND MELISSA SPOHN

THIS COLLECTION is based on a presentation by Melissa Spohn and John Whyde at the 1994 Virginia Hamilton Conference which provided an opportunity for participants to view the rich diversity available in media format. Additional film and video selections have been added along with CD-ROMs and World Wide Web addresses by Virginia Hamilton Advisory Board members from their own work with children and young adults, from award lists, and from reviewing available resources in public libraries and school library collections.

A potpourri of materials, the following selections include both information sources and fiction which represent a selection of some of the best multicultural materials that are "visually" available through film, video and through electronic formats. World Wide Web addresses were selected to extend the chapters contained in *Art and Story*. Selections such as CityNet and Lycos Maps extend geographical understanding by "visually" visiting a place that is familiar or unfamiliar. Each storytelling site provides a wealth of resources to extend stories and the Virginia Hamilton website represents the potential to learn more about an author her background through the biographical information provided, the "photo gallery," and the opportunity to correspond directly through e-mail.

All film and video entries are coded for age/grade level with a letter code following the entry. K-Kindergarten; P-Primary; I-Intermediate; J-Junior High; S-Senior High.

> *Abuela.* SRA, 12 min., 1994. (K-P)
>> Based on the book by Arthur Dorros, this fantasy adventure captures the story of a little girl and her grandmother as they fly through the skies over New York City and return to their home.

Lively Latin background music and the use of computer animation bring this video to life. A number of Spanish phrases are scattered throughout the narration.

Amazing Grace. Weston Woods, 10 min., 1993. (K-P)

Follows the story of Grace, who loves dramatic play, yet suffers a blow to self esteem when Peter Pan play auditions are announced. Though classmates, Say she cannot play the lead role because she is a girl and she is black, Grace is encouraged by her family and ultimately wins the role in this iconographic adaptation of Mary Hoffman's 1991 book.

American Women of Achievement: Wilma Rudolph. Schlessinger Video, 30 min., 1995. (I-S)

An informative overview of the life of legendary Olympian Wilma Rudolph which includes interviews with her former coach and teammates.

Arrow to the Sun. Films Incorporated, 12 min., 1989. (P-I-J)

Uses animation to tell the tale of the Acoma Pueblos about a boy's search for his father, detailing his voyage on an arrow to the sun. The boy undergoes trials in the sky village until he is recognized by his father, the Lord of the Sun. Based on the Caldecott Award-winning book by Gerald McDermott.

At the Crossroads. SRA/McGraw-Hill, 7 min., 1995. (P-I)

An iconographic presentation of Rachel Isadora's book about children waiting all night for their fathers to return from work in the mines after they have been away for many months. The video is enhanced by the narration and background music which reflect the South African culture.

Black Americans of Achievement: Collection II. Schlessinger Video Productions, 30 min. each, 1994. (I-J-S)

The second collection in this interesting and informative series that includes Muhammad Ali; James Baldwin; Mary McLeod Bethune; W.E.B. Du Bois; Marcus Garvey; Matthew Henson; Langston Hughes; Elijah Muhammad; Jesse Owens; and Alice Walker. Narrated by oral historian, John O'Neal, this series is adapted and follows the same format of a Chelsea House book series.

Children of Jerusalem. National Film Board of Canada, 29 min. each, 1993. (I-J)

A series of four videos including: Asya; Tamar; Neveen; and Yacoub which takes a look at the homes and lives of four children who live with the constant threat of political conflict. The children are from four cultures that make up the city of Jerusalem

A Common Goal. Eagle Multimedia Group. 14 min., 1994. (I)

Using the backdrop of young soccer players of different races and with flags of different countries represented on their uniforms for an opening, this video provides interesting and informative information about the United Nations. Visits made to sites around the world which emphasize the importance of being a team player to work out the world's problems as we work toward "a common goal."

Dancing in Moccasins: Keeping Native American Traditions Alive. Films for the Humanities and Sciences, 49 min., 1989.

An informative television documentary made available in video format which provides a history and perspective of the nearly two million Native Americans who belong to over 500 Indian nations.

Dr. Martin Luther King, Jr.: A Historical Perspective. Xenon Entertainment Group. 60 min., 1994. (J-S)

A documentary that follows the chronology of Dr. King's life and his political, educational and spiritual journeys. Includes recordings of his speeches and sermons, taped news footage and still photographs.

Eric Carle: Picture Writer. Searchlight Films/Putnam Publishing Group, 27 min., 1993. (P-I-J-S)

Features demonstrations of Eric Carle's signature collage techniques, while Carle speaks to the camera and in the background about the impact his teachers and family had early in his life which led to his successful career as an artist. This video was selected as the 1994 Andrew Carnegie Award winner.

Everybody's Different. Sunburst Communications, 14 min., 1994. (K-P)

This live action production with a multiethnic cast emphasizes appreciation of difference of talents, physical abilities and cultures. Special attention is given to promoting a positive self image to others.

Follow the Drinking Gourd. American School Publishers (SRA/McGraw Hill) 12 min., 1990. (I-J)

With illustrations from African folk tradition, this video is presented in story and song, based on the book by Jeanette Winter. Describing the story of Peg Leg Joe and a group of runaway slaves on their way to north to freedom via the Underground Railroad, Ron Richardson narrates and sings in this iconographic presentation.

The Great Kapok Tree. SRA/McGraw Hill, 10 min., 1995. (K-P)

Adapted from the book by Lynne Cherry, this video brings forth the importance of preserving the rain forest. A man plans to chop down a tree, but falls asleep at the base of the tree and different animals plead in his hear not to destroy their home. The iconographic presentation is enhanced with seemingly realistic sound effects of the rain forest, a number of different character voices and some animation.

Hailstones and Halibut Bones. Aims Media, 15 min., 1993. (K-P-I-J)

Mary O'Neill's classic and timeless collection of "color" poetry is presented through a variety of vividly intensive settings, a host of children and adults of different races and a lively musical background.

Here Comes the Cat! Weston Woods, 10 min., 1992. (K-P)

Based on the book of the same name, this is a collaborative Russian/American tale which provides inventive animation. It is enhanced with lively background music.

Holidays for Children Video Series. Schlessinger Video Productions, 30 min. each, 1994. (K-P-I)

A multicultural series of twelve videos that provides interesting information on twelve different holidays, including Kwanzaa, Rosh Hashanah and St. Patrick's Day. Includes a history of each holiday, a discussion of the symbols and customs, and suggested activities.

How to Fold a Paper Crane. Informed Democracy, 30 min., 1994. (I-J-S)

Opening with the legendary history of paper cranes, information about Sadako, and the Children's Monument in the Hiroshima Peace Park, this program provides very basic instruction to the 26 steps in folding a paper crane.

How to Make an Apple Pie and See the World. GPN/Reading Rainbow, 29 min., 1996. (K-P)

Features Marjorie Priceman's book about a little girl in search around the world for the very best ingredients for an apple pie. Includes a cooking demonstration with LeVar Burton and chef Curtis Aikens and further discusses some science connections in cooking.

In the Month of Kislev. Weston Woods. 13 min., 1994. (K-P)

An adaptation of Nina Jaffe's book (Viking Penguin, 1992) which provides information about the history of Hanukkah before beginning the holiday story of two families, a wise rabbi and a surprise ending. This story is based on a traditional tale and is presented with woodcut illustrations in an iconographic format.

Indians of North America Video Collection. Schlessinger Video Productions, 30 min. each., 1993. (I-J-P)

Each video provides an introduction to the unique history of particular Native American groups representative of different geographic regions of North America. Included are scholars discussing the history; on location visits to reservations; a presentation of issues; and an interesting look at each culture which is enhanced with photographs, film footage, music and traditional crafts.

Jackie Torrence Presents Stories from Around the World: African American Stories—Preschool and Kindergarten. National Training Network/Curriculum Associates, 27 min., 1996. (K-I-J)

Internationally known storyteller Torrence tells two African American folktales, "Wiley and the Hairy Man," and "The Old Woman Who Lived in a Vinegar Bottle" to a group of children. The performance is preceded by Torrence explaining the origin and development of African American folktales. The older age audiences are indicated because Torrence is an excellent storytelling model to watch when students are developing their own storytelling styles.

Jerry Pinkney: Meet the Caldecott Illustrator. American School Publishers (SRA/McGraw Hill), 21 min., 1991. (P-I-J)

A live action video which provides the rare opportunity to see Jerry Pinkney at work in his studio. Pinkney details the artistic process in creating a children's book including the research that goes into the drawings. (Another live action video of Jerry Pinkney, "A Visit with Jerry Pinkney," was released in 1995 from Dial/Puffin.)

Kwanzaa: A Cultural Celebration. Films for the Humanities and Sciences, 29 min., 1993. (I-J-S)

Presents the meaning and purpose of Kwanzaa, a holiday begun in 1966 during the Civil Rights movement, which is based on a Swahili word meaning harvest and was developed to encourage African Americans to develop a sense of community. Includes selections from established programs and suggests activities that promote the principles of Kwanzaa.

Last Breeze of Summer. Carousel, 30 min., 1992 (I-J-S)

Set in a Ranford, Texas, public school in 1957, this powerful story tells of a very determined young black girl, Lizzie Davis, who is the first to integrate the town's white high school to get the best education. A live action drama of a dedicated individual who grows up to become a teacher.

Mama, Do You Love Me. Story Time Associates, 13 min., 1993. (K-P)

The visual adaptation of Barbara Joose's 1991 picture book depicts an Inuit mother and child having a conversation which reaffirms the never ending love between them. An iconographic interpretation with some animation which is enhanced by background music of a flute and drum. The video provides a glossary to the Inuit words used throughout the work which is also included in the book.

Meet Ashley Bryan: Storyteller, Artist, Writer. American School
Publishers. 23 min., 1992. (P-I-J)

> Ashley Bryan shares stories, information about his life and work
> and a demonstration of his artistic process.

Multicultural Peoples of North America. Schlessinger Video
Productions, 30 min. each, 1993. (I-J-S)

> An extensive series which each highlights a particular culture
> that immigrated to America and describes their impact on
> today's environment. Each video details their journey to
> America, their contributions in their new country and looks
> indepth at one family. The series is based on the Chelsea House
> People of North America series. The selections include African
> Americans, the Amish, Greek Americans, Irish Americans, Jewish
> Americans, Korean Americans, and Puerto Ricans.

My Family, Your Family. Sunburst, 14 min., 1994. (K-P)

> A live-action video that features children of multiracial and
> multiethnic backgrounds in a variety of family situations.
> Questions about what makes up a family are included.

Paper Camera. New Dimension Media. 25 min., 1992. (I)

> Origami toys and baseball cards provide a language of their own
> in this story of a 10 year-old Chinese speaking Kwok and his
> English speaking friend Eric. This video demonstrates that
> language is not always a barrier to communication.

Patricia Polacco: Dream Keeper. Philomel. 23 min., 1996. (P-K-I)

> Polacco relates information about her life and her artistic process.
> Several of her works are highlighted and a demonstration of her
> artistic technique is shared.

Pool Party. Fast Forward, 28 min., 1992. (P-I)

> An invitation to a pool party provides young Rudy Herrera with
> an unusual chance to mingle with a well-to-do crowd very
> different from his own environment. Live action drama is the
> format for this 1993 Andrew Carnegie Medal winner.

Race to Freedom: The Story of the Underground Railroad. Xenon
Home Video, 90 min., 1993. (S)

> The story of four slaves who have escaped from a plantation in
> North Carolina and are trying to reach freedom via the
> Underground Railroad assisted by Harriet Tubman. A
> memorable drama with believable characters that provides a
> picture of their race to freedom.

Song of Sacajawea. Rabbit Ears Productions, 30 min., 1993. (I)

> The true story of the Lewis and Clark expedition through the
> Rocky Mountains to the Pacific Ocean led by their guide, a young

Shoshoni woman. An iconographic rendering that is enhanced with woodcut illustrations and a good musical score.

Squanto and the First Thanksgiving. Rabbit Ears Productions, 30 min., 1993. (P-I)

Actor Graham Greene narrates this presentation of the life of the Pawtuxet Indian who helped the Plymouth settlers toward their bountiful harvest which led to the celebration of the First Thanksgiving. An iconographic presentation based on impressive illustrations.

Virginia Hamilton: Meet the Newbery Author Series. American School Publishers (SRA/McGraw Hill), 20 min., 1992.

From her home in Yellow Springs, Ohio, Hamilton reveals the influences that her family and her love of the land have had on her career as an internationally acclaimed writer for young people. Ms. Hamilton shares family photos in her home, a visit to the elementary school she attended in Yellow Springs and an overview of her writing process.

Whitewash. Churchill Media, 25 min., 1994. (I)

The 1995 Andrew Carnegie award winning film for the best in children's video given by the Association for Library Service to Children of the American Library Association, this is the story of a young African American girl whose life is never the same after her face is spray painted white by a racist gang. Ruby Dee provides the voice of Helene's supportive grandmother and Linda Lavin provides the voice of her teacher. Helene is further assisted by her twelve-year-old classmates as they all come to grips with this traumatic event.

Additional video resources

An annual resource for selection of film and video is the compilation of the award-winning videos of the preceding year which is published each April in *School Library Journal*. Secondly, *School Library Journal* published a series of articles in six parts on Culturally Diverse Videos which was compiled by Phyllis Levy Mandell. The videos included were submitted by 400 publishers for inclusion and were published from 1985-1992   The articles included: Part 1, "African-Americans" (January 1992) pp. 49-65; Part 2, "Native Americans" (May 1992) pp. 63-69; Part 3, "Asian Americans" (September 1992) pp. 169-177; Part 4, "Hispanic Americans" (December 1992) pp. 65-72; Part 5, "Eastern Europeans" (May 1993) pp. 49-55 and Part 6, "The Middle East" (September 1993) pp. 172-175. A third additional source is an article by Alan B. Teasley and Ann Wilder titled "Teaching for Visual Literacy: 50 Great Young Adult Films." The article was published in the *ALAN Review* in Spring 1994, pp. 18-23.

WORLD WIDE WEB

These websites offer a rich and diverse collection of visual information sources that may be used by educators and students. Of course there are many, many more places to visit on the Internet. On the world wide web there are sites that offer information about authors, countries, recipes, music, directions for crafts, and so forth.

Following are just a few sites that may serve as beginning points (such as the Children's Literature Web Guide or Kathy Schrock's Guide for Educators). There are numerous other sites (such as the Virginia Hamilton or Patricia Polacco pages that provide direct information. Addresses were current as of January 1997.

A-Z of Jewish & Israel Resources

<http://www.ort.org/anjy/a-z/festival.htm>

Browse alphabetically or search the subject index for songs, dances and recipes.

American Memory Project from the Library of Congress

<http://rs6.loc.gov/amhome.html>

An excellent resource for students to explore the "memory" of the American people from the photographs of immigrants to turn of the century postcards to famous speeches from American history.

Black History Month

<http://www.netnoir.com/spotlight/bhm/index.html>

Among the rich details on this site there is information about African American history and Black History Month; African folktales; links to Afrocentric websites; and information about African American quilting.

Children's Literature Web Guide

<http://www.ucalgary.ca/~dkbrown/index.html>

THE site to locate information on children's literature on the web. This site has received numerous commendations. One section includes "Information About Authors and Their Books."

Citynet <http://www.city.net>

A comprehensive international guide to communities around the world with links to over 1,000 cities in over 200 countries.

Digital Tradition Folk Song Database

<http://pubWeb.parc.xerox.com/digitrad>

A database of the words to over 6000 folk songs from a variety of cultural backgrounds that are searchable by keyword, title and tune.

The 50 States of the United States

<http://www.scvol.com/states/fileindx.htm>

A page for locating state facts and general cultural information that provides over 800 links.

Guide to Museums and Cultural Resources on the Web

<http://www. lam.mus.ca.us/webmuseums>

Provided by the Natural History museum of Los Angeles County, this site invites you to take a virtual tour of all the continents and explore museums in each.

A Guide to the Great Sioux Nation

<http://www.state.sd.us/state/executive/tourism/sioux/sioux.htm>

This page details the rich history of the Great Sioux Nation, including links to landmarks, legends, artifacts, powwows, and customs.

I-Channel Ellis Island <http://www.i-channel.com/ellis/index.html>

Learn about the journey of people to America through the audio recollections of some of the immigrants who were among the more than 12 million individuals to enter the United States through Ellis Island from 1892-1954. Download some of the recipes from the cookbook and learn about what it was like to enter the country through Ellis Island.

Index of Native American Resources on the Internet

<http://hanksville.phast.umass.edu/misc/NAresources.html>

An index to a large number of Native American resources from legends to art to politics.

K-12 Electronic Guide for African Sources on the Web

<http://www.sas.upenn.edu/African_Studies/Home_Page/AFR_GIDE.html>

Information about Africa's languages, customs, governments, environment and people. Includes a Multimedia Archives with maps, images of animals, flags and satellite images and pictures of African masks.

Kathy Schrock's Guide for Educators

<http://www.capecod.net/Wixon/wixon.htm>

Contains over 800 links for educators which are classified into subject areas. This is a selection of sites that were found useful for enhancing curriculum and teacher professional growth. This site was created and is maintained by Kathy Schrock, a middle school librarian media specialist from Cape Cod, Massachusetts.

Kidlink <http://www.kidlink.org/home-txt.html>

An interactive site that has linked over 60,000 children from over

85 countries involved in a global conversation since 1990. Lots of possibilities for sharing a project with a class in another country.

Kwanzaa Information Center

<http://www.melanet.com/melanet/kwanzza/kwanzaa.html>

Provides a history of the holiday and meanings of the associated symbols.

Lycos Maps <http://lycos.com/roadmap.html>

This page provides a mechanism for finding addresses across the country and seeing them on a map that can be printed. This site will also provide a map and driving directions on how to get from here to there.

Patricia Polacco Page

<http://www.scils.rutgers.edu/special/kay/polacco.html>

Maintained by Professor Kay E. Vandergrift, contains biographical information about Polacco, a list of works by Polacco and professional articles about her work.

Virginia Hamilton

<http://members.aol.com/bodeep/index.html>

Features information about Virginia Hamilton. A full-color cover and annotations are provided for each of her works. Includes a list of forthcoming appearances, a photo gallery, a list of awards, and how to send e-mail to her.

Virtual World Tourist II <http://www.vtourist.com/vt/>

This homepage presents a world map that is clickable. Click on the continent or region for a closer map and once more to a country and then begin to search the websites that are located in that country or state.

Yahooligans <http://www.yahooligans.com>

A "junior" Yahoo index to hundreds and hundreds of kid-friendly sites arranged by eight general topics. Two of the general topics are "Art Soup" (which provides links to museums, dramas and dance) and "Around the World" (which provides links to sites related to culture, politics and history).

Additional Web resources

There are numerous books and articles in print which provide lists of the "best" web sites. A couple that we have found to be useful have been Jean Armour Polly's *The Internet Kids Yellow Pages, Special Edition.* (Osborne/McGraw-Hill, 1996) and the monthly column by Gail Junion-Metz in *School Library Journal* titled "Surf For." Junion-Metz's January 1997 column, focused on Black History Month and was titled "I Have a (Digital) Dream."

DISTRIBUTORS

AIMS Media
9710 De Soto Avenue
Chatsworth, CA 91311-4409

Carousel Film & Video
260 Fifth Avenue
New York, NY 10001

Churchill Media
6901 Woodley Avenue
Van Nuys, CA 91406-4844

Eagle Multimedia Group
91 5th Avenue, Suite 800
New York, NY 10003

Fast Forward/Gary Soto
43 The Crescent
Berkeley, CA 94708

Films for the Humanities and
Sciences
Box 2053
Princeton, NJ 08543

National Film Board of Canada
1251 Avenue of the Americas
New York, NY 10020

Rabbit Ears/BMG Kidz
131 Rowayton Avenue
Rowayton, CT 06853

New Dimension Media
85803 Lorane Highway
Eugene, OR 97405

Searchlight Films
Putnam Publishing Group
390 Murray Hill Parkway
East Rutherford, NJ 07073

SRA/McGraw Hill
220 East Danieldale Road
Desota, TX 75115

Storytime Associates
7108 S. Alton Way
Box 5185
Englewood, CO 80155

Weston Woods
389 Newtown Turnpike
Weston Woods, CT 06883

Xenon Entertainment
211 Arizona Avenue
Santa Monica, CA 90401

Fast Forward/Gary Soto
43 The Crescent
Berkeley, CA 94708

Films for the Humanities and
Sciences
Box 2053
Princeton, NJ 08543

National Film Board of Canada
1251 Avenue of the Americas
New York, NY 10020

Rabbit Ears/BMG Kidz
131 Rowayton Avenue
Rowayton, CT 06853

New Dimension Media
85803 Lorane Highway
Eugene, OR 97405

Searchlight Films
Putnam Publishing Group
390 Murray Hill Parkway
East Rutherford, NJ 07073

SRA/McGraw Hill
220 East Danieldale Road
Desota, TX 75115

Storytime Associates
7108 S. Alton Way
Box 5185
Englewood, CO 80155

APPENDIX C

VIRGINIA HAMILTON ESSAY AWARD

ESTABLISHED IN 1991, the annual Virginia Hamilton Essay Award recognizes a journal article, published in a given year, which makes a significant contribution to the professional literature on multicultural literature and multicultural literary experiences for children and young adults. Members of the Virginia Hamilton Conference Advisory Board select the winning essay from among the ones they nominate. The winner receives an honorarium and a plaque during the opening ceremonies of the Virginia Hamilton Conference.

As of the 1997 conference, seven essayists have received the award.

1991: "Recreating Black Life in Children's Literature," by Jean St. Clair. *Interracial Books for Children Bulletin*, 19: 3/4 (Fall/Winter, 1989), 7-11.

1992: "Teaching Multicultural Literature in the Reading Curriculum," by Donna E. Norton. *The Reading Teacher*, 44: 1 (September, 1990), 28-40.

1993: "A Balanced View of Acculturation: Comments on Lawrence [sic] Yep's Three Novels," by Mingshui Cai. *Children's Literature in Education*, 23: 2 (June, 1992), 107-118.

1994: "Issues in Selecting Multicultural Children's Literature," by Junko Yokota. *Language Arts*, 70:3 (March, 1993), 156-167.

1995: "Academic Guidelines for Selecting Multiethnic and Multicultural Literature," by Sandra Stotsky. *English Journal*, 83:2 (February, 1994), 27-34.

1996: "Against Borders," by Hazel Rochman. *The Horn Book Magazine*, 71:2 (March-April, 1995), 144-157.

1997: "Continuing Dilemmas, Debates, and Delights in Multicultural Literature," by Violet Harris. *The New Advocate*, V.9, No. 2, Spring, 1996.

APPENDIX D

ABOUT THE VIRGINIA HAMILTON CONFERENCE

ANTHONY L. MANNA

AS WE WERE putting together the final pieces of this book, the Virginia Hamilton Conference was moving into its thirteenth consecutive year. Back in the early 1980s had anyone told us that the conference we were thinking of establishing would become the longest-running event in the country to focus exclusively on multicultural literature for children and young adults, we would have been incredulous. For one thing, when the four of us who were teaching children's and young adult literature at Kent State University first came together in the early 1980s to discuss such a project, we were thinking about reviving the generic children's literature conference that had once been very popular on our campus, but had somehow gone to seed several years before. When we first came together, the farthest thing from our minds was a conference that would center solely on multicultural literature. This is not surprising. At the time, the momentum for what was soon to become a concerted effort among educators, librarians, critics, and publishers to lobby for more equitable representation of America's diverse cultures in literature for young people was just beginning to gather force. Compared to what we now have in the way of an ever flourishing multicultural literature market and the rich and varied discussion about theory and practice that responds to it, the early 1980s were relatively lean, uncertain years. For another thing, we weren't all that sure of finding sufficient financial support to keep any type of children's literature conference alive for very long. After all, the pedagogical movement known as whole language instruction, which endorses classroom experiences with a large selection of trade books, was still in its infancy. Needless to say, in the early 1980s, children's and young adult literature was not the hottest of topics nationally or locally, and multicultural literature was, comparatively speaking, just beginning to compete for wider and more serious attention.

While planning the conference at Kent State University, our attention turned to multicultural literature once we began to think about our potential audience. We weren't only imagining an audience of librarians, teachers educators, and students of literature, but an audience of children and adolescents whose good fortune it always is to find their way into good, honest books. Whenever the four of us who formed that first ad hoc committee met to discuss the shape the conference might take, we talked a lot about what literature can mean to kids, about how the best books captivate them, and once this happens, how the experience of reading and hearing and discussing books they love can not only help them understand their own lives a little better, but also can make them imagine the lives of others. Once we crossed the boundaries of our respective academic disciplines—library and information science, English, and education—and sat down at the same table to discuss how we might collaborate on this project, we soon learned that what we had in common was a strong belief that good books awaken you to the world around yourself and to the struggles, achievements, and, yes, the imperfections of people in other times and places. We knew that the stories and poems and nonfiction you read can even cause you to think about the misconceptions you may have about people who act, believe, and speak differently than you. We knew that the route to these discoveries is not paved with fervent, ponderous morals and lessons about tolerance, respect, and basic human decency, but with compelling stories about multifaceted and thus memorable and accessible characters involved in the messy business of living.

The conference now had a focus; it would center on cultural diversity in children's and YA literature. To explore this focus and the issues surrounding it, we intended to draw on the perspectives and experiences of authors, illustrators, publishers, librarians, educators, critics—anyone, actually, who makes good books available to young people. We had grand hopes about what would happen at this annual one-day event. Literature's potential for promoting cultural awareness and affirming cultural pride would be big concerns, but so would issues of community, of cultural defenses and boundaries, of the politics of inclusion and exclusion, and of the very real conflict over assimilation and heterogeneity that affects so many people who inhabit society's margins.

When it came time to give the conference a name that would broadcast its cultural theme and align it with provocative first-rate literature, we knew immediately that we should honor Virginia Hamilton. She is an Ohio native, and, having received nearly every major award and honor accorded American authors of literature for young people, she is also one of today's most prominent and critically acclaimed writers for children and young adults. As Betsy Hearne claims in *Twentieth-Century Children's Writers*, "Virginia Hamilton has heightened the standards for children's literature as few other authors have."

Once Ms. Hamilton consented to having the conference bear her name, she also accepted our invitation to inaugurate it, on April 12, 1985, by presenting the first keynote address. In that speech, she talked about the African American traditions that have influenced her work and traced her journey as a writer who explores the experiences of individuals within the context of their special cultural identity and history.

The program that followed Ms. Hamilton's speech set a precedent for how we would structure the conference for at least several years in the future. The 250 or so people who attended the first conference had a choice of two out of six workshops, which largely addressed literary elements in Ms. Hamilton's books and laid out practices for promoting multiculturalism through literature in classrooms. The workshops in turn were followed by a booksigning session with Ms. Hamilton.

Our audience generally reacted favorably to our first, tentative experiment in building a stimulating conference. One really positive assessment gave us good cause to carry on: "With the high level of scholarship presented, you have formed a touchstone event!"

MOVING TOWARD A COMFORTABLE FORMAT, OR WHAT'S IN A NAME?

Until 1988, the official title for the conference was "The Virginia Hamilton Lectureship on Minority Group Experiences in Children's Literature." As awkward and restrictive as that title now sounds, it does reveal what we thought back then about the issues that an annual forum of this sort should address and the cultures it should explore. For us, the purpose of a lectureship was to feature the work of a renowned author or illustrator whose very name evoked images of enthralling writing and art and brought to mind honest renderings of the lives and experiences of people from particular cultures. We wanted the insights of this talented headliner to drive the debate and discussion which we hoped the conference would engender.

It is indicative of our initial short-sightedness that we were working from such a limited notion of cultural diversity and a very conservative awareness of how far the landscape of multicultural literature might reach. In the early years of the conference, we thought that we should give most of our attention to people from racial and ethnic groups. And there was good reason for our way of thinking. Our sense of these matters had been shaped by the exciting and liberating promises and premises of the social, economic, and educational reforms of the late 1960s and the 1970s. With these struggles over civil rights and fair representation came poignant reminders of the fierce power struggle that keeps certain racial and ethnic groups in the margins, strips them of a voice, denies them their democratic rights, and threatens their dignity. In however small a way, the Virginia Hamilton Conference was aligned politically with these reforms and struggles. But it's not that we started with some noble political cause about settling society's wrongs. That would be like preaching to the choir. Rather, the politics accompanied the authors, illustrators, and other presenters who came to the conference to discuss the books they make, study, or read with their students. The politics came with the circumstances and conditions these books reveal, and this happened even when the books didn't intentionally make a cultural or political experience the center of attention.

It has taken a great deal of honest reflection and debate to align the conference with a concept of cultural diversity that embraces what we're truly after. What we've begun to understand, here in the late 1990s, is that a genuinely multicultural society—and a multicultural literature—should privilege all those individuals and groups whose history and daily lives and experiences, as Anne Haas Dyson and Celia Genishi put it in *The Need for Story* (National Council of Teachers of English, 1994), are rooted in "a shared way of interpreting the world." Once you begin thinking of human diversity in terms of the things that unite groups *within and across cultures*—things like basic human needs and drives, conflicts and struggles, language, religion, and customs, and ways of surviving and getting along in a family and making and losing friends and learning about responsibility, compromise, respect, and love—the multicultural cast increases.

This cast surely must include people of color and people of common ethnicity. But "ways of interpreting the world" also are shared by people of a certain age, gender, and class. And then there are people in particular neighborhoods, environments, regions, and times. And those trying to make their way through severe conditions and circumstances, people like the homeless and immigrants and survivors of war and holocaust... and the perpetually or terminally ill... and that large culture of young people with addictions... and the communities of gays and lesbians. And so forth.

Virginia Hamilton uses the term "parallel cultures" to describe this network of communities and groups. In the Foreword she wrote for *Many Faces, Many Voices* (Highsmith, 1992), an earlier book of conference proceedings, she explained what the term implies to her: "America is for me a country of parallel cultures rather than the more traditional, narrower view that portrays it as land of the majority surrounded by minorities. It is a country of parallel peoples, each creating a significant literature out of their own unique yet universal qualities. Therefore, it must be a land where all cultures and all ethnic groups are of equal value and of equal importance to our children, who are descendents of the world's peoples." By using the word "parallel," though, she's not suggesting that these cultures ought to live side by side and never meet the way parallel lines go on and on without ever touching. In fact, she means the very opposite. When she's asked about this—for example, in the interview with her in this book—she always points out that what she hopes to bring to mind with the word "parallel" are similarities and connections among cultures. She's talking then about crossing those cultural borders that Hazel Rochman so searingly touches upon, and she's referring to the ways people from different cultures can influence one another for the better by daring to resist barriers that would otherwise keep them isolated from each other.

Which brings us back to good books. We read them and we're carried out and away from our own world and transported to someone else's. When it comes to getting to know a different culture, a good book can be a great mediator. It places us squarely in the center of other people's lives, times, and circumstances, making them less foreign or distant or even threatening, and, to Virginia Hamilton's way of thinking, a lot more global. And if you stay alert during these excursions, you'll more than likely learn something about what you believe in and value and what you'd like to change.

In the first few years of the conference, we didn't have such a clear understanding of the rewards that multicultural literature can offer up. When we look back, we realize that much of what we have learned about multiculturalism and multicultural literature comes directly from the enormous talent and wisdom of the writers and illustrators who have served as our featured presenters. They would teach us a lot because their sense of things cultural is grounded in the special realities of the characters and situations they imagine into existence in their books. For example, at the second conference in 1986, author-illustrator Ashley Bryan wowed the audience with his enchanting style of performing a book by rendering its latent musical qualities. By doing this, he not only turned his presentation into a spirited jam session; he also showed us that to discover the voice of a text is one way to come in touch with the temperament of its culture—

in this instance, the African and Caribbean cultures—from which the text sprang.

Then, in 1987, there was Nikki Giovanni. In her characteristically candid manner of confronting touchy political issues head on, she explored the social and political realities of the African American children she portrays in her poems and made a vehement plea for respecting the rights of all children.

Walter Dean Myers gave the fourth keynote in 1988. In his splendid speech, he talked about his own personal history as a writer and how the subjects and themes he cares about are inextricably and deeply tied to the course of African American history. He said that for him the route to whatever is universal in the human world-wide community is discovered by tracking the particulars. Which particulars? For Walter Dean Myers, these are largely found in the experiences of city kids. That's the environment he knows and feels best; it's in his blood.

By 1989 we needed to revise the conference title. We felt that the solemn mood evoked by the term "lectureship" was out of synch with the main speakers' exuberance and stirring candor and the feeling of community that seemed to be growing among many of the people who came to the conference. If, as some of us believed, the term "lectureship" brought to mind stuffy, crowded classrooms, drowsy students, and a dry speaker, then it had nothing to do with the spirit of exchange and the wonderfully stimulating ideas about culture that the majority of the audience said the conference was generating.

Another thing that made the term "lectureship" fall short of the mark was a change we made in the program. This change was the performance with which we concluded the 1987 conference. Because we wanted to involve the audience in something moving and up-beat, we invited the Black Arts Ensemble of Cleveland's Karamu Theatre to perform *The Sweet Flypaper of Life*, an original musical based on the life and poetry of Langston Hughes. The play was so well received that we decided to make some type of performance one of the highlights of the conference. As it has become. Since 1987, we've offered storytelling concerts by Celestine Bloomfield, Jocelyn Dabney, and Joseph Bruchac, among others; a dance interpretation of multicultural poetry and stories by a youth ensemble from Michigan; concerts by a steel band and percussion group from Ohio's Central State University and by Kent State University's own African Music Ensemble; a program of readings of African American poetry, folktales, and spirituals by Ashley Bryan, whom we invited back for our tenth anniversary; and, in 1997, a celebration of poetry orchestrated by Poetry Alive!

We also felt that the term "lectureship" underplayed another vital source of information and energy at the conference: the six or so workshops that have enriched every program. These intense, one-hour sessions have, over the years, featured the insights of critics, educators, librarians, writers, illustrators, storytellers, historians, linguists, and many other professionals who've thought long and hard about cultural issues. Included among the provocative topics they've explored are the relationships among politics, curriculum, and pedagogy in classrooms and cultures, manifestations of cultural values and beliefs in contemporary and classic literature, gender issues in literature, interdisciplinary approaches to teaching multicultural YA books, the cultural significance of Hispanic musical forms, the transformation of myth and legend in Virginia Hamilton's works, cultural affirmation through literature for second-language learners, preserving a culture's history through oral traditions, using books to help meet the emotional and cognitive needs of chronically ill children, and practical strategies for encouraging kids to become engaged with the world of the book, think about discrimination and stereotypes in literature, art, and society, respect their own particular culture, and understand their connection with those from other cultures. This staggering array of topics could go on and on because we've had the good fortune to be led to a network of professionals from Ohio and throughout the country who come at culture from a very large number of perspectives. How could we not learn from these people?

When we did move to make a title change in 1989, we looked for a title that would do a good job of advertising the theme of the conference and of broadcasting what we had been learning about cultural diversity. We settled for the "Virginia Hamilton Conference on Multicultural Literary Experiences for Youth," and then later, in 1996, for the less verbose "Virginia Hamilton Conference on Multicultural Literature for Youth." We wondered whether labels like "festival" and "celebration" would better suit our purposes, but these seemed overworked, and while we wanted the conference to be festive and entertaining with regard to cultural affirmation—as it surely had become—we saw this as only one piece of the picture. Another piece focused on issues of artistic excellence and literary quality. And another revealed the thorny social and political issues that swirled around our project much of the time. Conflicts over segregation and integration is one of these issues. The dynamic between cultural similarities and cultural differences is another. And exploitation, oppression, and empowerment are others.

Just when it seemed that we had arrived at a comfortable format for the conference, we experimented with yet another major change in the program. At the seventh conference in 1991, we moved from featuring one speaker to several, and we structured this new development as a panel. We felt that this would be a good turn to take because it would allow us to headline a mix of writers and illustrators whose books represented various cultures and appealed to young readers of various ages. A panel could also include both established voices in children's and young adult literature and ones just making their way into these fields.

Our finances had a lot to do with this decision to feature several presenters. While the conference was by no means financially secure by 1991, it was no longer operating at a loss. One thing that helped make us solvent was an audience that we could count on. At both the fifth conference, which the novelist Mildred D. Taylor keynoted, and the sixth, at which the illustrator Jerry Pinkney was the featured presenter, we had reached audience capacity at 360 or so paid registrations. Simply put, we could afford to cover the cost of a panel's honoraria, accommodations, and travel expenses.

The first panel was a totally rewarding experience. Arnold Adoff, Ms. Hamilton's husband and an award-winning poet, took the role of moderator and also offered his views on the reasons for bringing poetry into a multicultural literary canon. Mr. Adoff shared the stage with Pat Cummings who, in a mesmerizing slide presentation on her books, led us through the stages of her development as a writer and illustrator, Sheila Hamanaka who, also with slides of her stunning work, talked about the process of putting together *The Journey* (Orchard), the book she both wrote and illustrated about the internment of Japanese Americans in detention camps in this country during World War II, and Nicholasa Mohr who, in an intriguing speech she called "A Journey Toward a Common Ground: The Struggle and Identity of Hispanics in the U. S. A.," candidly assessed the forces that have shaped her sense of what her culture means to her as a parent, citizen, and writer.

In their evaluations of the seventh conference, the audience had nothing but praise for our new format. Keep it, they indicated in almost all cases, and this is something we intend to do—while our finances hold out. Since 1994, the panel has been our modus operandi. With it, we've been able to showcase an astonishing range of wonderful, stimulating talent. The panel roster now includes, in the order of their appearance, Floyd Cooper, Brian Pinkney, Vera B. Williams, Shonto Begay, Lulu Delacre, Joyce Carol Thomas, Patricia Polacco, James Ransome, Jacqueline Woodson. Jan Spivey Gilchrist, Eloise Greenfield, Ted Lewin, and Pat Mora.

FUNDING THE CONFERENCE

Trace the history of this project and you soon see that the Virginia Hamilton Conference will keep evolving only to the degree it has adequate financial backing. And as we have learned over the years, you are successful at eliciting sufficient financial support only to the degree you can prove your credibility and have a reputation for making a difference. The conference is, after all, a business.

However obvious these principles may seem in retrospect, it has taken those of us who have managed the conference from the beginning much trial-and-error to learn them. Sixteen years ago, we launched the project with a zero balance, hoping that our paid guests would see us through the first lean years. Even though we are solvent today, we still are as cautious and concerned about the status of our finances as we were in the early 1980s. And we still are in the time-consuming business of looking for support from organizations within the university community and outside of it.

What exactly are the sources of revenue for a project with an annual expenditure of close to $16,000? There are three principal sources. The first and most reliable are the conference registrations. The current registration fee is $65. It includes a continental breakfast, a luncheon of international foods, a conference packet, free parking, a choice of two workshops from among eight or nine, and attendance at all presentations in the main auditorium: the panel of featured speakers, Ms. Hamilton's annual "Reflections," and the final performance.

A second source of revenue are agencies and organizations in the community. The Cleveland Foundation and the George Gund Foundation, also in Cleveland, provided funds to help get us started, and the Victor C. Laughlin, M.D. Memorial Foundation Trust, another foundation in the Cleveland area, and Hamilton Arts, Inc. have been contributing to the conference since 1989. Local public libraries also have supported the project over the years. These include the Akron-Summit County Public Library, the Cuyahoga County Public Library, and the NOLA Regional Library System. Finally, a number of publishers—including Greenwillow, Putnam, the now defunct Macmillan Publishing Co., and Highsmith Press—have offered support by helping to cover miscellaneous expenses.

Constituencies within Kent State University also have been an important funding source. These range from academic departments to the university's bookstore.

As the university faces increasingly severe budget cuts, it makes fewer and fewer contributions to projects like ours. The message it now consistently gives is to seek funding from external agencies.

The project took a productive financial turn in 1992 with the publication of the conference proceedings. All revenue from the sale of the first volume of proceedings, titled *Many Faces, Many Voices: Multicultural Literary Experiences for Youth* (Highsmith), is being used to help support the conference. The same arrangement has been made for this second volume.

When you itemize its many expenses, you can't help but see how costly an undertaking the Virginia Hamilton Conference truly is—if you want it to be known as a superior event that shouldn't be missed. For a start, consider the cost of these indispensable items: round-trip travel, honoraria, and accommodations for featured speakers and workshop presenters; a quality brochure that's mailed to approximately 4,000 prospective participants; bookmarks, a recent, successful strategy for advertising the conference; equipment rental; and rent for using the university's conference center (a surprise to many people).

Had we known sixteen years ago how expensive it would become to maintain the conference and what a determined effort it takes to keep it solvent, we probably would have abandoned the project. Part of the project's allure, though, is surely the determination it takes to keep it alive. This has a way of forcing you continually to reflect on and reaffirm your belief in your cause. The thing that keeps our belief in the conference strong is knowing that there are people in our audience who will become inspired to lead kids to books that open their minds and help them understand their connection with others a little better.

MANAGING THE CONFERENCE

That no amount of money is going to rescue a project like the Virginia Hamilton Conference from bad management is another one of those elementary lessons we've learned by default. Those of us who established the conference took it for granted that it was our responsibility to manage every aspect of it—until, that is, we ran smack-face up against the problems that come from having too much to do too soon.

The help we needed came in several forms. In 1987, for example, we began to cooperate with the bureau on campus that is known for its expertise in managing successful conferences. Although one condition of this agreement requires us to use a sizable portion of our annual profit to pay for this service, working with the folks in the bureau has been in the long run a cost effective development. For one thing, better management has meant that we now have in place an efficient and consistent plan for advertising the conference. For another, it means a well organized program on the day the event takes place. There's no doubt that more effective outreach and a more smoothly run program have helped attract more people to the conference and keep them coming back each year. There's profit in that. In any case, our business colleagues, adept at such matters, keep the conference on task on time.

The conference took another turn toward improved management in 1987 when we formed an advisory board. Our intention was to seek the advice of people who spend a good amount of their professional time in literature's realm, studying and celebrating books and thinking of exciting ways to hook kids on reading. What we did was to put together a team of a dozen or so school and public librarians and classroom teachers who work with kids of all ages. By joining us, they committed to attending monthly meetings where, among so many other things, they would plan conference programs, consider sources of financial assistance, and develop strategies for attracting people to the conference.

As it turns out, though, the advisory board's contribution is far more complex than attending to details that can make the conference operate efficiently. This is the case because the board's discussions always come back to the claims and aims we're making about multicultural education in general, and, in particular, about multicultural literature. It seems there isn't a board meeting that goes by where we don't consider what multiculturalism means and which cultures need to be represented at the conference. Whenever our discussions turn to building worthwhile conference programs, we usually wind up wondering about how it's possible to promote multiculturalism without avoiding a Cook's tour approach where you cover a lot of cultural territory without ever stopping long enough in any one place to learn anything of any value. Which books give that impression, we've often asked ourselves? Which books, on the other hand, encourage an in-depth journey? The board members continue to be such a powerful force in shaping the conference and our understanding of multiculturalism that it's hard to imagine how those of us who established the conference ever survived without the privilege of their convictions. Of all the insights the board's work has revealed, perhaps the most important is this: You only can begin to embrace a genuinely multicultural perspective on the world beyond your own when you refuse to privilege one cultural group above others. This may not seem much of a startling discovery to others, but to us it has opened the way to many important issues. Consider, for example, how long it has taken many of us who probably should know better to extend the multicultural range so that includes, along with people of color and people of common ethnicity, all those groups that experience "a shared way of interpreting the world." Even today you can read a large stock of commentary about multicultural literature for young people and still find definitions of culture that exclude rather than include, that set up walls and barriers while at the same time promising to show you how *multi*cultural books promote *multi*cultural awareness. Whose culture? Which culture?

Where the board is today about multiculturalism has been a long and sometimes hard journey. Anyone who has attended its meetings since the board first came together in 1987 will be able to lay out a long list of doubts, quandaries, and, of course, significant realizations. One realization that currently is driving us once again to assess how we might enter a culture through a good book is Omar Catañeda's provocative proposal for what he calls an "Aesthetic of Estrangement" (*CBC Features*, Spring-Summer, 1995). What he means by this is that, as readers, we'll probably do a better job of coming to an understanding of a culture if we "...value the unfamiliar above identification, teach the joy of displacement, and relish a sense of disquietude." In other words, to enter the culture in a book and come away understanding it may not be as easy as some people would have us believe. It can be a wonderfully entertaining and exhilarating experience, but it can be a challenging one as well.

Exploring and acting upon ideas like these is one of the great rewards of collaborating with the keenly sensitive and perceptive folks that agree to serve on this board. If the conference is like a well-run machine, the engine is the advisory board.

FACING THE ISSUES

Part of the allure of managing the Virginia Hamilton Conference is surely the complexity of so fascinating a phenomenon as multicultural literature. The challenge of understanding the political, social, moral, and aesthetic forces and issues that influence and shape this literature is what makes our project such seductive work.

We end this introduction to the conference by identifying five critical issues that guide our work and cause us the most concern about multicultural literature. We do this with the hope that these issues will evoke as much reflection on multicultural literature among those who read this book as they have among those of us involved in the Virginia Hamilton Conference.

1. *What is the meaning of the term "culture" and how does the term apply to literature and other arts? Which groups and individuals are embraced by the meaning you give the term?*

   Over the years, we've learned to see multiculturalism as a complex mix of identities and affiliations. But where do you draw the line? Should you draw the line? Is every group a culture? How responsible are we for making sure that all cultural groups are somehow included in multicultural literature programs and curriculums in libraries and schools?

2. *How is it possible to endorse an equitable representation of cultures without running the risk of promoting a multicultural Cook's tour?*

Teachers and librarians who attend the conference tell us that managing a relatively inclusive program of multicultural literature is problematic. It is tempting to translate this responsibility into a need to treat each culture as a separate, isolated experience. Coverage can mean superficial treatment, to say nothing of failing to recognize cross-cultural connections and borrowings.

3. *How important is it to achieve a balance between acknowledging cultural differences and affirming cross-cultural similarities, between focusing on the things that make a particular culture unique and the things that tie it to other cultures?*

The danger in exploring the special or unique is making the culture appear so completely strange and exotic that it's not a place we'd care to visit for any length of time and certainly not a place where we'd learn all that much. On the other hand, focus on the universal and you may wind up using the culture as a safe harbor for personal identification and therefore for what you already know and care about, without really getting to know the culture with any depth.

4. *How do you know if the author's or illustrator's rendering of the culture is accurate and authentic?*

Once upon a time, we thought that criteria for considering accuracy and authenticity would mostly be helpful to people who are outsiders to the culture that's represented in a book. Our experience with students and the conference participants tells us otherwise. The problem, though, is that lists of criteria alone are not very helpful; if you don't know the culture very well how can you distinguish between, say, type and stereotype, and how can you detect subtle misrepresentations in values, beliefs, relationships, language patterns, and so forth? What we need are applications of the criteria by critics who have an insider's perspective on the culture, and we need these insider critics to create resources that offer honest, readable appraisals of contemporary and classic cultural books. We need more resources like Rochman's *Against Borders* (American Library Association), Sims's *Shadow and Substance* (National Council of Teachers of English), Slapin and Seal's *Through Indian Eyes* (New Society), Cart's *From Romance to Realism* (HarperCollins), Schon's *A Hispanic Heritage* (Scarecrow), Robertson's *Portraying Persons with*

Disabilities (Bowker), and Kutenplon and Olmstead's *Young Adult Fiction by African American Writers, 1968-1993* (Garland).

5. *Can writers and illustrators provide an accurate and authentic portrait of a culture that, officially speaking, is not their own?*

The insider/outsider debate is surely one of the most intense contemporary controversies among writers, illustrators, critics, and publishers. We enter the fray whenever we set out to plan a conference program that promises a range of viewpoints about cultural representation in books for young people. Regarding our choice of featured presenters, the issue of accuracy and authenticity is always less of a problem than the national debate would have us believe. After all, the community of writers and artists we draw on is made up of people whose reputations precede them—as demonstrated, for instance, by the awards and honors they receive from professional organizations whose exclusive or main purpose is to feature authentic and accurate cultural literature. But more to the point of the insider/outsider debate is this significant fact about the conference: not all of the authors and illustrators who have spoken at the conference are bonafide members of the cultural communities they depict in their books.

While we don't recommend using book awards as the sole test of whether a writer or illustrator—or, for that matter, an editor or publisher—got everything right, the practice does remove a lot of the guess work from the issue of accuracy and authenticity. What's more, when in doubt, we can always do what anyone who recommends or selects cultural books can do: use reputable resources that tell you whether writers and authors of young people's literature really know a culture. In any case, we never expect one artist or writer or workshop leader to present the entire cultural picture. After all, his or her voice is just one among many, and his or her interpretation, in this particular book, focuses on just one aspect of cultural experience from among many.

We do not mean to dismiss the importance of this issue. We know of the gross inaccuracies and blatant misrepresentations that can creep into books that look and sound beautiful. Yet, our discussions about which writers and artists do it best always seem to come back to the same rule of thumb: Judge not the accuracy or authenticity of a cultural experience in a book—or film, CD-ROM, or performance—only by some rigid rule about the author's or illustrator's cultural membership. Rather, judge it by how adept this particular author or illustrator is in this particular book—or film, CD-ROM, or performance—at leading you toward some significant awareness of how these people in their particular circumstances and conditions are living out their lives.

SUBJECT INDEX

TITLE INDEX

(v) Denotes film and video titles.

AUTHOR/ILLUSTRATOR INDEX